SAINTLY SUPPORT

SAINTLY SUPPORT

*A Prayer for
Every Problem*

Produced by The Philip Lief Group, Inc.

**Andrews McMeel
Publishing**

Kansas City

03 04 05 06 07   TWP   10 9 8 7 6 5 4 3 2 1

Library of Congress Cataloging-in-Publication Data

   Saintly support : a prayer for every problem / produced by the Philip Lief Group, Inc.
       p. cm.
     Includes index
     ISBN 0-7407-3336-2
     1. Christian patron saints—Prayer-books and devotions—English. I. Philip Lief Group.
BX2166 .S25   2003
242'.8—dc21   2002043181

Produced by The Philip Lief Group
Senior Editor: Judith Capodanno
Writer: Hope Gatto
Editorial Assistant: Marybeth Fedele
Photo Researcher: Sally Wilson
Book Design: Annie Jeon
Book Composition: Kelly & Company, Lee's Summit, Missouri

CONTENTS

INTRODUCTION

For all of us, life is peppered with triumphs and conflicts, big and small. Some days are glorious examples of all that is right in the world—a promotion, a new baby, a clean bill of health from the doctor. Other days are riddled with nagging problems we just can't shake—a sore tooth, lost keys, a sick pet. But more than likely, as it has been for centuries, most of our lives are filled with a bit of both. And through the years of everyday problems mixed with good fortune, one thing has remained constant: at times we feel the need to search for help from beyond our realm. Sometimes, we can look only to God for answers and aid. But what is the best way to make sure our pleas for solutions and blessings are heard? Ask the saints.

Returning to the age-old tradition of requesting the intercession of the saints on our behalf, this book helps anyone enlist the assistance of the saints by asking them to pray both with and for you. Because of the saints' closeness to God and their Christian purity, their prayers can be especially effective.

Asking the saints to pray for us is a practice that dates back to the earliest days of Christianity. When Peter was in prison, "prayer by the church was fervently being made to God on his behalf" (Acts 12:5). Paul realized the power of collective prayer and frequently asked his fellow Christians for prayers of support. In his letter to the Romans, for example, Paul appealed to his brothers and sisters "to join me in the struggle by your prayers to God on my behalf" (Romans 15:30). Of course, these prayer requests were asked of living Christians, but why not seek the help of Christians who have come before us?

Who Are the Saints?

The definition of *saint* has changed over the years. In many versions of the Bible, several New Testament passages use the word *saint* to refer to those who believe in Jesus and follow his teachings, regarding all Christians—living or dead—as saints. Today, the word is reserved as a term of reverence for a very select group of Christians. The more restrictive definition of *saint* was initiated by the early Church leaders as they sought to honor those Christians who had shown an extraordinary passion for the teachings of Jesus during their lives and were known to reside with God in Heaven. The process they established for determining sainthood is called canonization; the term was taken from the Greek *kanon*, meaning a measuring tool or standard of measurement. Because the early martyrs had made the ultimate sacrifice for Jesus, they were the first to be canonized as saints. Eventually, the standard was broadened to include those who had led exemplary Christian lives.

In the first centuries of the canonization process, sainthood was determined by popular acclamation, but later the task became the responsibility of the bishops. A feast day, usually the date of the candidate's death, was assigned within the diocese to celebrate the saint's life and good works. Bishops would occasionally confer with the pope on canonizations; and by late in the tenth century, it was determined that the decision to elevate someone to the status of saint was of such importance that it should be the province of the Church's supreme authority. The first papal canonization for which there is definite documentation is that of St. Udalricus in 973.

Today, there is a strictly structured system for canonization. Canonization does not even begin until many years after the death of a candidate. Following the nomination, a panel of theologians at the Vatican thoroughly investigates the candidate's life for proof of holiness and/or martyrdom. The pope declares the candidate "venerable," or sacred, once he or she has been approved by the panel and the cardinals of the Congregation for the Causes of Saints.

Veneration and Beatification

The next step on the path to sainthood is beatification, which (except in the case of martyrs) requires evidence of a miracle that can positively be attributed to the candidate's intercession. The ability to perform miracles is considered proof that a saint is indeed in Heaven and can intercede on our behalf, so the miracle must be performed as a direct result of a prayer request after the candidate's death. Once beatified, or blessed by the pope, the candidate can be honored by a province or diocese, but one more proven, documented miracle is required before the pope will elevate the candidate to the status of saint.

Patronage

It is no wonder then that people have been turning to these sanctified souls for help in getting their requests to God's ears. And the saints' patronages guide us to the specific causes that were of particular import to the saints when they were alive. Many of the saints have been granted the additional designation as a patron, or guardian. The tradition of assigning patronage is as old as the saints themselves, and is determined by the special circumstances of the saint's life. St. Antony of Padua, for example, is regarded as the patron saint of lost articles because a missing prayer book was recovered following his impassioned prayer. St. Vincent de Paul is honored as the patron of charities because of his devotion to the poor and needy. A saint may serve as the patron of several "specialties" according to his or her experiences. St. Udalricus, the first saint to receive papal canonization, is not only the patron saint of weavers but is also invoked by those seeking relief from fever, frenzy, and faintness, as well as from mice and moles.

Friends in Heaven

Just as having friends on earth to whom we can turn gives us strength and comfort, so can our relationships with Christians who have come before us. Life is eternal, so while our relationships with loved ones take on a new dimension after death, they certainly do not have to end. We frequently talk with departed relatives, sharing good news and bad and seeking their support and guidance. We can have similar relationships with the saints. Some of us may even have favorite saints, those with whom we feel a special bond, perhaps because our problems are similar to those they experienced during their earthly existence. Others we turn to in prayer according to their patronage when a special need arises.

As we turn to the saints in prayer, we honor their memory and recognize their unity with God. We do not pray *to* them; rather, we ask them to pray to God with us and for us, just as we would ask a close friend or relative for their prayers. As Paul says in chapter 3 of Ephesians in the New Testament: "God is able to do exceeding abundantly above all that we can ask or think," and what better way to ask than through the prayers of the saints?

The Patron Saints
and the Prayers

Abuse

St. Monica

Feast Day: August 27

The Mother of St. Augustine of Hippo, Monica was born in the fourth century in North Africa to a devout and disciplined Christian family. An arranged marriage created by her parents matched her with Patricius, a very determined man who was said to have an uncontrollable temper. The situation got worse when Monica's belligerent and irritable mother-in-law came to live with the couple after the wedding. Her husband and his mother abused Monica verbally, if not physically, and the mistreatment she endured in this living situation led to her patronage against abuse. In the end, Augustine, Patricius and her mother-in-law converted to Christianity under Monica's influence.

St. Monica, dedicated mother and stalwart wife,
Pray for those who are in dangerous situations.
Ask the Lord to give those who are being mistreated and battered
The courage to protect themselves and their children.
Pray for the little ones who are abused and neglected
So that God's love will give them
Peace and comfort during their darkest days.
Amen.

AIDS Patients

Aloysius Gonzaga

Feast Day: June 21

A noble of Italian heritage, Aloysius Gonzaga studied to be a soldier and aristocrat from the time he was four years old. He was still quite young when he was bedridden with a form of kidney disease, but he considered this to be a blessing, as it gave him ample time to devote to quiet prayer. When Aloysius turned eighteen, he surrendered his worldly possessions to his brother and joined the Jesuit order. During the plague outbreak of 1591, Aloysius was a twenty-three-year-old religious student who tended to plague victims in Rome and then succumbed to the plague soon after. He is considered the patron saint of AIDS patients because of his dedication to those suffering from disease and fevers.

O dear Aloysius Gonzaga,
You have witnessed with your own eyes the suffering of innocents.
You have been afflicted with the fever of compassion.
Please intercede on our behalf to comfort and heal the patient before us.
Fill our hearts with courage to survive trying days,
Engulfing our hearts with rapture
For the love of God and the Holy Heavens.
Amen.

Alcoholism

St. Martin of Tours

Feast Day: November 11

A cavalry officer who rarely saw combat, Martin was also known as "The Merciful" for his refusal to do battle. He left the military and became a hermit, dedicated to holiness. He attracted other monks and they formed a Benedictine abbey, where they worked diligently preaching and converting locals. Consecrated bishop of Tours in 372, he moved to a hermit's cell that became the foundation of a new monastery. Martin was prone to visions and able to invoke the willpower to go on lengthy fasts. Perhaps this determined focus is what led to his patronage of alcoholism and reformed alcoholics.

Oh, Sacred Heart of Jesus,
I pray for the willpower and the attentive direction of St. Martin.
I ask for this obsession to be lifted and for You to provide the strength
To continue living my life one day at a time.
I do not know what tomorrow brings,
But give me the courage today to walk away from temptation.
With Your love and companionship, Lord, I will stay humble.
Amen.

Animals

St. Francis of Assisi

Feast Day: October 4

Francis of Assisi had a wayward childhood spent street fighting and getting into scrapes. His errant behavior led to some time in jail, and while there he believed he received a message from God. After he was released from prison, Francis was determined to be more religious. The young Italian dressed in shabby clothes, begged for food and served the sick and poor. His dedication to preaching led him to start the Franciscan order in 1209. He spent the remainder of his holy life caring for lepers, feeding the hungry and cleaning churches. Because he lived among wildlife and had a special bond with all of God's creatures, Francis of Assisi is considered the patron saint of animals.

St. Francis of Assisi, lover of animals,
Pray with me for the well-being and safety of the beasts of the world,
Ask God to remind us to cherish the tiny lives we are responsible for.
Pray that children will grow up tolerant, compassionate
And respectful of our animal friends.
St. Francis, please ask our Heavenly Father
To guide more people into charity work for abused and unwanted animals.
Amen.

Armed Forces

St. Maurice

Feast Day: September 22

Also known as Mauritius, Maurice was a layman and a Christian officer in a band of soldiers from Upper Egypt. During the reign of Emperor Maximian around the year 287, there was a huge massacre in what is now Switzerland. Approximately 6,600 men were killed in a giant sweep by their own troops because they refused to take part in pagan sacrifices prior to their scheduled battle. Maurice was one of the brave leaders who defended his religion and gave his life for his faith on the battlefield. He is often represented in paintings as a knight in armor with a red cross on his breast, which is the badge of the Sardinian Order of St. Maurice.

O brave St. Maurice, you gave your life on your own battlefield
for your faith.
Keep all soldiers in the palm of your hand
So that they may make the right decisions in times of war.
May they be brave in the face of God.
May they feel love when they are afraid.
May the armies of the world show mercy before they show fear.
We ask you to pray especially for the soldiers
We hold dear in our hearts.
Amen.

Arthritis

St. James the Greater

Feast Day: July 25

James was a fisherman when he was called by Jesus to preach the Gospel of the Lord. A brother of John the Apostle, he is thought to have also been a cousin of Jesus. Of the two disciples named James, this James became an apostle first, and that is why he is called "the Greater." One legend that surrounds James involves a boy who had been hanged unfairly. Although the boy had been dead for over a month, James brought him back to life. When the boy's father was told of the miracle, he scoffed and said that his son was as dead as the roasted bird he was about to eat for dinner. Just then, the bird proceeded to stand up, grow back its feathers and fly away. This invigorating story may be the reason James is considered the patron saint of arthritis. He was the first apostle to be martyred when he was stabbed in Jerusalem at the age of forty-four.

St. James, prayerful man and hard worker,
I ask for your prayers with respect and love.
Pray to God our Father for the suppleness of these limbs to return.
Ask God to take away the stiffness of bones, aching back and
hardness of joints
So that I may tend the gardens of my life with His love and support
And without pain and difficulty.
I humbly ask for your solemn prayers.
Amen.

Artists

St. Luke the Apostle

Feast Day: October 18

Luke was born a pagan slave and became one of the earliest converts to Christianity. He was a doctor by profession, but legend says that he was a magnificent painter who did portraits of Jesus and Mary. Luke was also a talented writer. He wrote some of the most well-known parables from the New Testament, such as those about the prodigal son and the good Samaritan. For his interest in the arts, Luke is considered the patron of artists in all media and is sometimes depicted in art holding a painting of the Virgin Mother.

Dear and loving St. Luke,
Ask God to bless my eyes as I paint,
Hold my hand as I write,
Open my ears as I make music.
Let your creativity inspire my work
So I am able to fall into a rhythm of vision.
Ask God to bless all artists
So they may create under His loving hand.
Amen.

Athletes

St. Sebastian

Feast Day: January 20

In the late third century, Sebastian joined the Imperial Roman Army. Despite his position as a Roman officer, Sebastian comforted the victims of Emperor Diocletian's persecution of the Christians. Because of his humanitarian efforts, he was accused of being a Christian as well. Tied to a tree, brutally besieged with arrows and left there to die, Sebastian freed himself and fully recovered from the vicious attack. Diocletian finally had him beaten to death. Later, when the Black Death was taking lives in the fourteenth century, villagers prayed to St. Sebastian for safety when the arbitrary "arrows of nature" caused outbreaks of the plague.

Dear Commander at the Roman Emperor's court,
You chose to be a soldier of Christ and spread faith in the King of Kings—
For which you were condemned to die.
Your body proved athletically strong and the executing
arrows extremely weak.
May athletes have the same strength of body, mind and spirit
To help them reach new heights and achieve their goals.
Amen.

Babies

St. Brigid of Ireland

Feast Day: February 1

B rigid, also known as Brigit and Bride of the Isles, was born to a pagan Scottish king and his Christian slave in 453. As a young girl, she had a big heart and could not bear to see suffering and hunger. She gave away the milk from her father's dairy, yet the business prospered. Her father arranged for her to marry, but Brigid quickly went to a beloved bishop and took vows to keep her virginity. Later, she was given her freedom and became a great traveler and started convents all over Ireland. Brigid has many patronages but is known to intercede on behalf of children through her own optimism and innocence.

Beautiful St. Brigid who offered milk to the poor,
Please pray for this child to be nourished by God's love.
Please pray for this child to be safe and protected
All the days of his/her life.
Embrace the innocence of this tiny soul,
Offering strength and warmth during times of weakness and cold.
With your tender heart, keep this child's fate in the palm of your hand.
Amen.

Bachelors

St. Casimir of Poland

Feast Day: March 4

Casimir was third in line for the throne when he was born in 1458. A Polish prince and grand duke of Lithuania, Casimir was a severe and regimented man. He refused the luxury of a comfortable bed and slept on the ground, spending most of the night deep in prayer. He chose to be celibate for life, committing himself to be a devoutly religious bachelor. He was pressured to marry the emperor's daughter, but Casimir stayed true to his promise to God. The single prince was devoted to the Virgin Mother and assisted the poor during his honorable life.

St. Casimir, entreat God with arms open wide,
To embrace bachelors like yourself.
Offer them comfort and warmth, support and strength.
May they be guided by the love of their family
And may the affection of their friends lead them
To a serene happiness that can only grow within.
Amen.

Bad Weather

St. Médard

Médard was born in the middle of the fifth century in Picardy, France. He was ordained a priest when he was thirty-three and subsequently became one of the most adored and highly recognized bishops in northern France. It is believed that when Médard was younger, he was once protected from bad weather by an eagle that flew right above his head. This legend led to his patronage of good weather and against bad weather, called upon by those who work outdoors. It is also said that whatever the weather is like on his feast day, it will be so for the next forty days.

St. Médard, entreat the Father of the Heavens and of this earth
To protect us from bad weather
Just as He protected you in your time of need.
Ask Him to comfort us with sunny skies,
Cool us with soft breezes,
Warm us with His love and sunlight.
Please help keep this important day free from unexpected downpours
And shelter us from all storms.
Amen.

Blindness

St. Odilia

Feast Day: December 13

Odilia was born blind to a Frankish noble family in the seventh century. Her father resented her for her disability and gave her away to peasants. She lived with a poor family until the age of twelve, when a convent took her in. While being baptized by Erhard of Regansburg, a future saint, she was suddenly able to see, and the news of the miracle spread. Her brother heard that Odilia's blindness had been cured and had her returned to her family for use in an arranged marriage. Her father was so angry at his son's greed and embarrassed at abandoning his daughter that he killed his son. Odilia fled back to the convent and remained true to the faith that had healed her. She became an abbess and founded the Odilienberg Monastery.

O blessed St. Odilia,
I beseech thee to pray for a continuing vision,
A strong and clear sight,
So that I may bear witness to the beauty of God's world.
May I always remember that my heart can see things my eyes cannot
And often those are the most beautiful of images.
Amen.

Body Purity

St. Agnes of Rome

Feast Day: January 21

In the middle of the third century, right before she was to become a teenager, Agnes was ordered to make a sacrifice to pagan gods and to give up her virginity. She was supposedly taken to a temple and led to the altar, where she made the sign of the cross. She was then tortured for refusing to deny her love for God. She refused to marry any of the several men who offered themselves and retained her virginity. Sources vary as to the way in which she died, but it is definite she was murdered for her beliefs.

Dear and sweet Agnes of Rome,
Please pray for all the young people
Who are pressured into adulthood too early.
Lord, give them the courage and the strength to stay true to
The beliefs of their parents, the Church and themselves.
Keep them pure, O Lord,
Until the time is meant for them to marry.
Amen.

Breast Cancer

St. Agatha

Feast Day: February 5

Alovely and wealthy girl, Agatha was an early Christian who devoted her life to the service of God. When the edicts were announced against the Christians and they were persecuted, Agatha became the victim of blackmail. She was told that if she worked as a prostitute in a brothel she would not be charged. Agatha protected her purity and refused to accept customers, rejecting the cruel advances of powerful men. For this she was tortured and thrown in jail, where her breasts were cut off. There are other stories that claim she was then healed by St. Peter. Agatha continued to be tortured over hot coals until a destructive earthquake dispersed her captors. The Italian maiden died a martyr and thanking God for an end to her pain.

Pure maiden of Sicily,
You were tortured to the core of your womanhood.
Pray that I have the same courage as I fight the raging battle
within my body.
In the Lord's name, ask that I may be brave in this struggle,
Strong in will and determined in spirit in the face of illness.
Let me remember your sturdiness when I am feeling weak.
Amen.

Burglary

St. Leonard of Noblac

Feast Day: November 6

Leonard of Noblac came from a family of Frankish nobles and became a member of the court of King Clovis I. Once, when an invading army was charging the kingdom, the queen asked Leonard to call upon God to help them defeat the approaching soldiers. Leonard prayed and Clovis emerged the victor. A bishop then easily converted Clovis, Leonard and many others, using the battle as an example of God's power. The nobleman left the court and later entered a monastery but soon realized that he craved a more solitary life to devote more time to prayer. He retreated into the woods, leaving only to go to church. Others pleaded to live with him in his holy place in the forest, and a new monastery was created. Leonard of Noblac's patronage against burglary may stem from his success in warding off the theft of King Clovis's kingdom.

St. Leonard of Noblac,
Protector of kingdoms, lover of peace,
Pray that our home is kept safe from intruders.
Guard our house with the power of God's love.
Keep all that dwell within these walls safe from all evil
And all we've worked so hard for safe from theft.
Amen.

Burns

St. John the Apostle

Feast Day: December 27

John the Apostle was considered to be so close to Jesus that he was called *the beloved disciple*. A fisherman and brother of St. James the Greater, John was in attendance at the Last Supper and stayed true to Christ until the end, praying at the foot of the cross as Jesus died. After the crucifixion, John took Mary, the Blessed Mother, into his home and cared for her as her protector. It is said that Emperor Domitian had John beaten and hurled him into a pot of scalding oil only to have John emerge untouched. For this reason, John the Apostle is considered the patron saint of burns.

Blessed Apostle John, beloved disciple,
Pray for a recovery from the fire that burned.
Pray for protection from the heat of evil that can burn our souls.
The pain can be so great, thus we beseech you to pray for our relief.
You were a friend to Jesus in his time of need.
We turn to you for protection from blazes
And for a healing done in His name.
Amen.

Businesspeople

St. Homobonus

Feast Day: November 13

Homobonus was born the son of an Italian tailor in the beginning of the twelfth century. His father gave him an education in running an effective and honorable business. The tailor's teachings were put to good use when Homobonus inherited the business upon his father's death. Married, with several children, Homobonus looked upon his honest work as a way of serving God and his family. He gave much of his money to the poor and his time to helping the needy. After he turned fifty years old, Homobonus gave up his trade and spent his days deeply committed to charity. Then one night, while attending his daily evening mass, the holy businessman threw his arms in the air in the sign of the cross and fell dead. He was immediately honored as a saint, and his cult spread quickly.

Beloved and charitable St. Homobonus,
Your honesty and good will served your community and the Lord well.
Help me follow your example and not give in
To temptations of greed and easy shortcuts that wound others.
I ask for guidance in my work, so that I may prosper
By choosing virtue over avarice.
Amen.

Cancer

St. Peregrine Laziosi

Feast Day: May 1

Peregrine Laziosi was born in 1260 in Forli, Italy, to a very wealthy family. His youth was spent selfishly and was monopolized by material possessions. He found his way into politics and became very anti-Catholic in his beliefs. Peregrine converted, however, after beating Philip Benizi, a future saint, and seeing the holy man turn the cheek and pray for his attacker. Peregrine later joined the Servite order and spent many years in solitude. The gentle confessor fell victim to a horrific cancer of his foot that spread rapidly. While awaiting amputation, Peregrine spent the night before the operation in prayer and had a vision of Jesus healing his malady instantly. By the next morning, his foot was completely cured.

O great Peregrine,
I am inspired by your faith, bravery and stamina.
Pray that I can be as strong and prayerful as you were.
Ask God to get me through this painful experience
with dignity and laughter.
Pray for my supportive family and my loving friends
As God sees me through to a total recovery.
Amen.

Charities

St. Vincent de Paul

Feast Day: September 27

Vincent de Paul was born a peasant in southwest France in 1581. Extremely bright, Vincent received his education from Franciscan friars and then became a tutor to noble children in town. He spent some time at the University of Toulouse and became a priest when he was twenty years old. Vincent found that his best work was done when he worked for the poor. He championed the needy by creating many organizations that nursed the sick, fed the poor and found work for those who were struggling to provide for their families. Vincent de Paul was dedicated to serving those in his community who were abandoned, enslaved or desperate for the love of God.

Dear and noble St. Vincent de Paul,
Inspire all charitable workers, especially those who minister to the poor,
To surround those in need with the grace of our Lord.
Bestow upon these blessed servants the strength to continue
Until the hungry have been fed and the sick have been nursed.
When they tire, let them rejoice in the knowledge
They are doing the awesome work of the Lord.
Amen.

Child Abuse

Ss. Alodia and Nunilo

Feast Day: October 22

Alodia and her sister, Nunilo, lived in ninth-century Spain with their Christian mother and Muslim father. After their father's death, their mother married another Muslim, but this new stepfather treated the girls horribly and abused them unmercifully because they were Christians. They escaped the wrath of their stepfather and went to live with a Christian aunt, promising God they would dedicate their lives to Him and never marry. Although persecution of Christians was on the rise, the girls refused to renounce their faith, and they were later beheaded. The abuse they endured by their stepfather makes them patron saints of children who are in dire need of protection.

Beloved sisters who have suffered so much,
Please offer your prayers to the innocent souls who are living in fear.
Pray for their courage, their safety and their will to survive.
Give them emotional support through God's love and protection.
Ask our Lord to bring those they fear to justice so that
These beautiful children can know a life without horror.
Pray that the persecutions of young victims
End at the sound of this prayer.
Amen.

Childbirth

St. Margaret of Antioch

Feast Day: July 13

Soon after Margaret was born, her mother died and her father, a pagan priest, disowned her. A Christian nurse adopted her, and Margaret was raised a devout Catholic girl. One day when she was a young woman, a Roman prefect tried to seduce her and Margaret turned him down. The Roman accused her of being a Christian and had her arrested. When she also refused to sacrifice to the pagan gods, the authorities attempted to kill her with fire, but Margaret's prayers kept her from being burned. Other stories have Margaret being swallowed by a dragon and escaping when the holy cross she kept with her irritated the dragon's insides. Because of this legend, Margaret of Antioch is associated with labor and pregnancy.

For the safe delivery of a new baby,
I ask you to pray, St. Margaret, for an uncomplicated birth.
Bless the womb of this strong mother
And pray for the health of this unborn child.
Please cradle the pair and their loved ones in your knowing arms
While asking the Lord to protect them from harm.
In our Savior's name we pray.
Amen.

Childless People

St. Anne

Feast Day: July 26

Anne was the mother of the Virgin Mary. For many years, Anne and her husband, Joachim, tried desperately to conceive a child. She promised God that if she were to bear a child she would dedicate the baby to God's service. One day while Joachim was gone, an angel visited Anne and informed her that God was listening to her prayers and she would have a child like no other. Soon after, Anne gave birth to Mary and, as promised, she devoted her daughter to God. Anne's faithful dedication to God during all the years she yearned to have a baby has made her an inspiration to those hoping for a child and to expectant mothers.

St. Anne, dedicated mother of the Blessed Lady,
You understand the pain and anxiousness of wanting a child.
Help me to be strong in the face of God's plan for me.
Pray that I remain accepting of whatever news is in my future.
Pray with me, St. Anne, for a miracle to arrive
And pray with me that my trust in God remains constant.
In the Lord's Almighty name, I pray.
Amen.

Children

St. Bathild

Feast Day: January 30

When Bathild was a young girl in England, she was kidnapped and sold to French royals as their slave. When she matured, she married King Clovis II in 649 and went from slave girl to queen. When Clovis died, her sons were too young to rule, so Bathild assumed power until the oldest came of age. Even with this new huge responsibility, Bathild remained deeply devoted to her children. She set a good example for her young princes by using her position to serve the Church and aid the needy. She forbade the persecution of Christians and donated money to create monasteries and churches. In 665, her son Clotaire took the throne, and Bathild spent the rest of her days in a convent praying and tending to the sick.

Saint and Queen Bathild, from slave to royal, you spent
your days dedicated
To serving your children and those around you.
I ask in the Lord's name for you to pray for these children
So that they may grow up to be blessed, strong
And confident members of God's Church.
May they be offered the same support you granted your own sons
And find peace and happiness all the days of their lives.
Amen.

Church Unity

St. Cyril

Feast Day: February 14

Cyril was born of Greek nobility connected with the senate of Thessalonica, although his mother may have been of Slavic descent. He was also the brother of St. Methodius. He took the name Cyril upon becoming a monk and made it his mission to convert others to Christianity and bring unity to the Eastern and Western churches. He was sent to convert the Jewish Khazars of Russia and came back to Greece with great success and a mastery of their language. He also developed an alphabet for the Slavonic language that later became known as the Cyrillic alphabet.

St. Cyril, Apostle of the Slavs,
I request your prayers to unite all churches in peace and serenity.
Help us pray for harmony among all churches and all religions.
Allow communication to be endless and constant.
Allow voices to be heard and understood.
Pray in the name of the Father, that our churches in both the East
and the West
Stand forever and ever in honor and virtue.
Amen.

Clergy

St. Thomas Becket

Feast Day: December 29

Thomas was born in 1118 in London and grew up to become a lawyer, soldier and then archdeacon of Canterbury. The young King Henry II chose Thomas as his chancellor, one of the most powerful subjects in the kingdom. They became close friends, and Thomas was at times just as celebrated as the king himself. After much pomp and lavish ways, Thomas began to feel he had lost his way as he drifted further and further from a religious life. He stripped himself of luxury and gave himself to fasting, hair shirts, vigils and constant prayer. He resigned the chancellorship and became a devout clergyman. After several rifts with the king, Thomas was finally martyred in the cathedral at Canterbury in 1170.

St. Thomas of Canterbury,
Pray that our priests and our nuns remain steadfast in their
Faith and devotion to the Lord.
Ask God to bless our deacons and
All the laypeople who work hard for our parishes.
May your holy example inspire our good servants to be strong.
Amen.

Cold-Weather Protection

St. Maurus

Feast Day: January 15

Maurus was born in either the sixth or the seventh century to a Roman nobleman named Equitius. His father thought it best for the boy to begin his education at the age of twelve and entrusted him to Benedict, a future saint and a wonderful spiritual teacher of the time. Benedict grew very fond of the boy, and when he came of age, he named Maurus as governor of Subiaco. Legend has it that one day a boy named Placid fell into a lake and was taken away by the current. Benedict saw this in a vision just as it was happening and called for Maurus to rush out and save him. Maurus then miraculously walked across the chilly waters and heroically pulled the boy to safety. Today, Maurus is called upon as a protector against the cold.

St. Maurus, friend of Benedict, brave hero to Placid,
I call on you at this moment to pray for the protection
Of those who are cold and afraid.
Warm them with your holy prayers made possible by God's power.
I entreat you to ask the Lord to please take the chill from their bones
And replace it with the healthy affection of God's love.
Amen.

Colic

St. Charles Borromeo

Feast Day: November 4

A nephew of Pope Pius IV, Charles became a lawyer at the age of twenty-one. He suffered from a speech impediment, but it did not stop him from becoming a cardinal at the age of twenty-two and archbishop of Milan just two years later. Also known as the Apostle to the Council of Trent, he fought diligently to enforce the decrees of the council and for peace. Despite his heavy load of duties in church politics, Charles never forgot the needy, especially the children. He founded schools, hospitals and many Sunday schools. His lifelong dedication to children's needs may be the basis for his patronage of colic.

Pray for this child, St. Charles Borromeo,
That peace finds its way into this baby's body.
Ask God to give strength and patience to this child's parents
While they gently rock their child to sleep.
Ask Him to instill the calm of the Holy Spirit into this tiny body.
Pray for all loving parents who need extra strength
When they are tired and desperate.
Amen.

Converts

John the Baptist

Feast Day: August 29

John was a cousin of Jesus Christ and began his ministry around his twenty-seventh year. He gave up all worldly goods to spread the word of the coming Savior. He survived during his travels by eating locusts and wild honey. John brought many new believers to the Christian faith. Later, he baptized into the Lord his cousin Jesus and then told his own disciples to follow Christ. Herodias beheaded John because of the words of a jealous and wicked woman; his head was brought to her on a platter. John was then buried in Samaria.

Dear Baptizer of the Lord,
I ask for your strength
As I try to spread God's word in my own small way.
When I speak of my newfound love for the Lord to others,
Let them feel the dedication and respect in my heart.
Give me the fortitude to be a good Christian and help me help others
Come to know and accept Christ as well.
Amen.

Coughs

St. Quentin

Feast Day: October 31

Quentin was a third-century French martyr and the son of Zeno, a Roman senator. He converted to Christianity later in his life. It is thought that sometime during the reign of Maximian (286–305), Quentin traveled into Gaul as a missionary to preach to and convert the Belgic peoples. The end came for Quentin when he was arrested on the basis of his religion and then viciously tortured. After being decapitated, his body was disposed of. Astonishingly, it was recovered a great deal of time later and Quentin was given a proper and simple burial. Through the years, miracles, especially cures of coughing spells, have been said to have taken place at Quentin's tomb.

Dearest St. Quentin and martyr for our faith,
Through our prayers to the Lord God,
Ask for a healing of this relentless cough.
Please implore our Lord to cleanse the body
And offer a calm throughout.
St. Quentin, I pray for a peaceful relief through your blessed intercession.
Amen.

Cramps

St. Pancras

Feast Day: May 12

Pancras, or Pancratius, was an orphan when his uncle brought him to Rome at the age of fourteen. Not born Catholic, Pancras converted to the faith and became associated with Nereus, Achilleus and Domitilla, other future saints. Pancras was put to death during either the Christian persecutions of Valerian (257–258) or Diocletian (304–06). A church built over his grave in the fourth century still stands today in Rome, although it has been altered over the years. Perhaps due to the manner in which he died, calling upon St. Pancras is thought to help those suffering from cramps.

O St. Pancras, boy martyr and brave Christian,
Please join me in prayer to relieve the pain.
Ask the Lord our God to ease my body's discomfort
And replace the hurt with tranquillity.
As your suffering was faced with great faith, St. Pancras,
I confront my affliction knowing God is full of mercy.
Amen.

Disabled People

St. Seraphina

Feast Day: March 12

Seraphina lived in poverty her entire life, yet she always found a way to help other needy and desperate people in worse situations. She lived as a recluse in Italy, doing chores and tending to the disadvantaged, spending each night in prayer. She suddenly contracted a condition that made every movement painful and impossible. Seraphina could only travel by being carried, motionless, on a board. The resilient young girl lived out the rest of her life in suffering and neglect but offered everything up to God through prayer. She was also devoted to St. Gregory, who had a physical condition very similar to hers. Seraphina's many physical challenges never lessened her love for Christ.

St. Seraphina, you were strong through your weakness,
In glory through your pain.
May your example inspire those who are challenged
to realize their opportunities for love and success, grace and happiness.
Pray they are accepted equally in God's Church and our community.
Keep their faith shining brightly in the dark.
Amen.

Disasters

St. Genevieve

Feast Day: January 3

Represented in art as a shepherdess because of her protective spirit, Genevieve prophesied dramatic events in Paris, from military invasions to natural disasters, and shielded the city through prayer. It was believed that she could read the consciences of those around her and offer peace to those possessed by the devil. When the Franks attacked the famous French city, Genevieve strove to get food to those in need and arranged for a network of prayers to be said for protection. In 1129, over six hundred years after she died, her relics were transported through Paris, and many believed the event ended an epidemic of disease at the time.

Shepherdess of Paris and imploring protector,
Please use your petitions to defend against catastrophe.
Shield us from natural and man-made disasters
Through the glory of your words to God.
Keep us safe from all that could harm us
In the scope of Heaven and Hell.
Pray for the safety of the masses in the name of the Lord.
Amen.

Doctors

Ss. Cosmas and Damian

Feast Day: September 26

These Arabian twin brothers studied the sciences in Syria in the third century and went on to practice medicine. They accepted no money from their patients and were considered two of the *anargyroi*, saints venerated for refusing payment for their services. Cosmas and Damian made their faith obvious to those around them, and this made them a clear target once Christian persecutions began. They were arrested and then beheaded. Many healing miracles have been associated with the men. After the death of the brothers, people spent the night in their church in Constantinople and were visited by the saintly physicians. They awoke healed of their sickness and disease.

Holy and loving Cosmas and Damian, I pray for the
blessing of all physicians
So that their hands are steady, their minds are sharp,
And their dedication remains constant.
Aid them in their commitment to healing
And provide them the strength and wisdom to continue
Their demanding profession.
In God's name, I pray.
Amen.

Dogs

St. Hubert of Liège

Feast Day: November 3

The grandson of a king and the son of a duke, Hubert was born in eighth-century Holland and grew up in the sophisticated world of royalty. He was extremely fond of hunting and decided to forgo church on a Good Friday to hunt instead. He pursued a stag and was astonished to see a crucifix between the animal's horns. The animal turned to Hubert and told the hunter to devote himself to the Lord. Hubert dropped to his knees immediately before the stag and went on to become a dedicated Christian and bishop for many years. His closeness with animals, especially hunting dogs, is the basis of his patronage of dogs.

St. Hubert of Liège,
I beseech your prayers for all canines.
May they be cared for by loving owners.
I ask you to pray for my own pet
Who is a devoted and unselfish member of this family.
Ask the Lord to bless the abandoned dogs
And guide them to loving and capable homes.
Amen.

Earache

St. Cornelius

Cornelius was a priest who may have belonged to a great Roman family. He was chosen as pope after the death of Fabian in 250. There were differences in thought as to how Christians should be treated after they had denied their faith during persecutions and then wanted to return to the religious community when it was safe. Cornelius took a very forgiving approach to the matter, while others were much more harsh. He was a proven listener to opposing views. He died in 253 as the Christian persecutions flared up again.

St. Cornelius of Rome,
I ask you to pray for relief of this earache.
Ask the Lord our God to remove the discomfort
For he has healed so many who approached Him in need.
As a great listener, Cornelius,
You paved your way to a place in Heaven.
I pray unto God to follow the same path.
I pray for the Lord's healing hand to be placed upon my head
While I give all glory to Him.
Amen.

Earthquakes

St. Emydigius

Feast Day: August 5

Greatly honored in Italy, Emydigius' true history is not really known. It is thought he was a German convert who went to Rome in the fourth century. He was passionate about his religion and is said to have rushed into a temple and smashed pagan statues of gods to the ground. This angered the pagans greatly. He had to be saved by Pope Marcellus, who sent him away to evangelize another region. Emydigius was later beheaded during the Diocletian persecution along with three of his companions, who would also become saints. He is considered the patron saint of earthquakes, possibly because of his smashing the giant stone statues in the temple.

Patron of earthquakes, dear St. Emydigius,
I ask for your intercession in keeping the earth calm.
Pray to God that our houses and our families
Stay safe in a turbulent world.
Ask for the Lord's blessing to maintain tranquillity
When the ground begins to tremble.
Amen.

Epilepsy

St. John Chrysostom

Feast Day: September 13

John was very well educated and was raised by an extremely holy mother in the fourth century. He became a monk, preacher and priest. John's sermons were so powerful that he was given the name "Chrysostom," which means golden-mouthed. He harped on the rich for not sharing their wealth and he believed that there should be fidelity in marriage. He worked diligently to reform the clergy and heralded just and charitable causes. Certain nobles and bishops did not like what John had to say and he was removed from his diocese and exiled. He died soon after. The patron saint of epilepsy, John may have suffered from the condition in his lifetime.

Golden-mouthed priest of Antioch,
I ask for your prayers in dealing with this affliction.
Please help me live a life not controlled by the uncontrollable.
Give me guidance in managing this illness
And take away the fear that walks by my side.
Through prayers to our Lord, ask that this condition
Be made easier through a cure or through intervention.
In the Lord's name, I ask for your help.
Amen.

Eye Problems

St. Lucy

Feast Day: December 13

L ucy is believed to have been born in Sicily in the beginning of the fourth century, to a wealthy, noble family. She was raised a Christian and wanted very much to give her fortune away to the poor and devote herself to the Lord. During the Diocletian persecutions, a Roman soldier attempted to rape Lucy and she tore out her own eyes in front of the attacker rather than surrender to him. She was ultimately arrested, tortured and killed for her faith. In art, Lucy is often shown offering her eyes to her attacker. For this reason, she is the patroness of eye trouble. Similarily, her name is connected with light and her feast day is celebrated as a festival of light.

Sweet and virtuous St. Lucy,
My eyes are failing and your prayers are needed.
I pray for the gift of sight
So that my life is brighter to serve the Lord.
Ask the Lord to take the soreness and blurriness away
So that I may see God's vision more clearly.
St. Lucy, I ask for your intercession
So that I will be blessed with light.
Amen.

Falsely Accused

St. Dominic Guzman

Dominic Guzman was born into a noble Spanish family in 1170. When his mother was pregnant with him, she had a vision of a dog with a torch in its mouth setting the world ablaze with the flame. Later, this same image became a symbol for the *Dominican order*, which Dominic founded in 1215. The order was based on living a simple and holy life with supreme dedication. After a while, Dominic grew discouraged that his mission was not expanding the way he wanted it to. He then received a vision from the Virgin Mary, who showed him a wreath of roses and told him to recite the rosary. His patronage is of the falsely accused.

Dear St. Dominic Guzman,
I respectfully ask for your intercession through prayer.
Please ask God to guide me through this situation.
Ask our Heavenly Father to support me as I have been falsely accused.
Ask Him to give me the right words, do the right things
And take the right defense as I stand up to my accusers.
In the Lord's name, with your help,
I pray for my name to be cleared and my innocence proven.
Amen.

Family Happiness

St. Dympna

Feast Day: May 15

Dympna was born to a pagan Irish chieftain and a wonderful Christian woman. When her mother died, her father, Damon, set off to find a new spouse. He could not find anyone as lovely as his wife and turned his affections to his daughter. Dympna fled his lewd advances and ran to Belgium, where she was hidden by Gerebernus, a family friend and priest. Her father found her and murdered Gerebernus. Dympna refused to give in to him and he killed her as well. She is often depicted in art as a princess holding a lamp and a sword.

Sweet and brave St. Dympna,
You endured so much from your abusive father.
I beseech your prayers so that happiness finds my family.
I ask the Lord to take away all bitterness and fighting
So that we may protect and love one another as families should.
I ask, in God's name, for a family strength that we can all count on.
Amen.

Famine Prevention

St. Walburga

Feast Day: February 25

Walburga was a daughter of Richard, an early king of England (also a saint), and grew up to give her life to God. She became a nun and spent her time with a few companions, converting pagans in what is now Germany. She died in Germany at the age of sixty-nine after a successful lifetime of spreading the Word of the Lord. Her relics were moved on May 1, the date of a pagan festival that celebrates the beginning of summer. She is also represented with three ears of corn, which may be one of the reasons she is the patroness against famine and for good harvests.

St. Walburga, servant of the Lord our God,
Your prayers to God are clear and strong.
I ask that you pray for a good season for our farmers
And that the world maintains a plentiful supply of food.
I ask God to bless all who are hungry, especially the children.
Please provide those in need with the tools and means to survive.
Teach us how to make the most of God's bounty
So famine may disappear from the face of this wonderful earth.
Amen.

Floods

St. Christopher

Feast Day: July 25

His name meaning "Christ-bearer," Christopher was a large man who sought adventure. He once met a man who lived as a hermit beside a treacherous stream and told travelers about the safest places to cross the body of water. Christopher was taught about God by this hermit and decided to follow in his footsteps. The new Christian even physically carried people across the stream on his mighty shoulders. One day, Christopher carried a child across whose weight was overwhelming. After the trip, the child turned into Christ, bearing the heaviness of the world. Christopher is considered the patron of travelers and against floods.

O powerful St. Christopher,
Ask the Lord to protect us from the streams and rivers that overflow.
Ask Him to guide the currents away from homes and families
And give us your strength
To carry the power of God on our shoulders.
Please help keep the water at bay and God's grace overflowing.
Amen.

Foot Problems

St. Servatius

Feast Day: May 13

Servatius was born in the fourth century to Armenian parents. He became one of the staunchest supporters of Christian orthodoxy and fought intensely for validation of his beliefs. He was named bishop of Tongres in Belgium and took his post very seriously. He took part in many councils, where he fought for the good of prevailing attitudes in Christianity at the time. Servatius also prophesied that Attila the Hun would invade Gaul. The vision came true the year of the saint's death. It is thought that perhaps Servatius had serious foot or leg problems, leading to his patronage of these afflictions.

St. Servatius, your visions and light
Gave you strength to endure through battles.
I ask for your important prayers in this battle I fight.
I pray for God's will to heal my feet and return their mobility.
I ask you, St. Servatius, to pray for God's blessing of health.
Amen.

Forgiveness

St. Mark the Evangelist

Feast Day: April 25

Mark was a relative of Barnabas the Apostle and is thought to be the Mark who wrote one of the four Gospels. When he was younger, Mark traveled with Paul and Barnabas on a missionary journey that brought the teachings of Jesus to lands far away. It is said that during this journey, Mark had a falling out with Paul and left the two men to preach alone. But Mark suddenly returned to Jerusalem and worked out his differences with Paul. It is because of his forgiving nature and apologetic spirit that Mark is considered the patron of forgiveness.

St. Mark the Apostle,
Friend to Peter and servant of the Lord,
I ask you to pray for me so that I may see
The faults I've brought to friendships
And the pain I've caused in relationships.
Help me find true forgiveness in my heart
And pray that I am gracious enough
To accept the apologies of others.
Amen.

Good Weather

St. Clare of Assisi

Feast Day: August 11

On July 16, 1194, Clare was born in Assisi, Italy. Clare heard Francis of Assisi preach in the town and she confessed to him that she wanted to devote her life to Christ. Soon after, Clare left home and took her vows. She founded the *Order of Poor Ladies (Poor Clares)* and headed the order for four decades. Pope Innocent IV wrote, "O wondrous blessed clarity of Clare! In life she shone to a few; after death she shines on the world! On earth she was a clear light; now in Heaven she is a brilliant sun."

St. Clare of Assisi, who brought sunshine to all you met,
I ask you to pray for agreeable weather for my special intention.
Please beseech the Lord to keep the storms and clouds away
On this special and wonderful day.
You radiated brilliant light upon those who knew you.
I pray, O Clare, to the Lord for clear skies above.
Amen.

Headaches

St. Stephen the Martyr

Feast Day: December 26

Not much is known about Stephen except that he was a deacon and the first martyr. The Twelve Apostles called a meeting and decided to create deacons to help with preaching, baptizing and distributing food. Stephen is mentioned as the first of the deacons. He was a powerful speaker and was known to speak with such vigor that he angered the elders of synagogues. After an exceptionally potent speech about the murder of Christ, he was taken out of the city and stoned to death around the year 34. He is often represented in art with stones on his head, suggesting his patronage of headaches.

St. Stephen, you gave your life speaking out about the crucifixion,
I ask that you pray for my own pain
As I need help getting through my suffering.
With His blessing, ask that my head be kept free of aches and stings
So that I may focus on taking care of friends, family
And spreading the joy of His love.
Amen.

Head Injuries

St. John Licci

Feast Day: November 14

John's mother died in childbirth in 1400, and he began working miracles from his infancy. When his father left John alone while working in the fields, a neighbor woman heard John crying. She brought John home and laid him next to her paralyzed husband, and miraculously he was cured immediately. When John was returned to his father, the husband became paralyzed again. John devoted his life to God and continued working miracles throughout his life. A renowned healer, John cured at least three people with head traumas before dying at the age of 111. He wore the habit for ninety-six years, longer than any other clergyman.

St. John Licci, healer and friend to the community,
I beseech you to pray for these wounds to mend.
Restore to health this poor soul who has so much to give to the world.
By the grace of the Lord,
Pray for the restoration of this injury
And steady the doctor's hand throughout the healing process.
With God's blessing, I implore your help.
Amen.

Heart Patients

St. John of God

Feast Day: March 8

John was born in Portugal in 1495. To the dismay of his parents, at the age of eight he followed a traveling priest and was later taken in by a count and educated. John tried different careers as a soldier and a salesman until he heard John of Avila preach about suffering and joy. John went into a frenzy and ended up in the hospital, where he stayed and took care of the patients. He then ran his own organized hospital in constant prayer with God. For thirteen years, John took care of the sick, sheltered the homeless and prayed with all of his heart. He became ill from years of overworking his body and died on his knees in prayer on his fifty-fifth birthday.

John of God worked diligently for the sick,
Dedicating his heart to the Lord's service.
I pray to God in Heaven to bless the heart of my loved one,
Keeping it strong and healthy.
Let this heart beat with the power and the love of God,
Making the body stalwart and sound.
In the Lord's name I pray.
Amen.

House Hunters

St. Joseph

Feast Day: March 19

The adoptive father of Jesus Christ and spouse of the Blessed Virgin Mary, Joseph was a strong and loving man who provided well for his family. Hundreds of years ago in Europe, nuns seeking more lands for new convents were encouraged to bury their St. Joseph medals in the ground. Through St. Joseph's intercession, miracles occurred and the lands were obtained. Today, those seeking a smooth real estate transaction have buried small statues of St. Joseph in their yards. After the house is bought or sold, the statue is retrieved from the ground and put in a place of glory in the new home.

Dear St. Joseph, household protector,
Please pray for a trouble-free house sale.
Pray that a loving family is welcomed by this home
And that a seamless settlement is completed.
Please ask that we find the perfect house to move into and
That it becomes a peaceful dwelling for our family.
In the Lord's name, we offer our thanks.
Amen.

Illness

St. Teresa of Avila

Feast Day: October 15

Teresa grew up studying the lives of the saints and even as a young girl strove to be like them. She would pretend and play "hermit" in the garden of her Spanish home. At a young age, Teresa was crippled by a disease and was educated at home; however, she was completely cured after a prayer to St. Joseph. She left home at the age of seventeen without telling her father and entered a Carmelite house. Not long after she took her religious vows, Teresa became extremely ill, and her sickness became worse because she did not have the proper medical help. She would never see a complete recovery. She died in 1582 as a gentle woman blessed with holy visions.

Oh, sweet St. Teresa of Avila,
You understand the heavy heart of sickness.
I ask for your prayers so that I see a complete recovery.
Ask our Father in Heaven to take away this illness
And shower me with good health and spiritual strength.
St. Teresa, my faith is strong in your gentle prayers.
Amen.

Infertility

St. Fiacre

Feast Day: August 30

Fiacre was raised in a monastery in seventh-century Ireland, where he learned how to use healing herbs. He became well known for his intelligence and his deep faith, and people congregated around him. Seeking complete holy isolation, Fiacre fled to France and established a hermitage. According to legend, he asked the bishop there for land to grow a garden of healing herbs. The bishop offered him as much land as he could plow in one day. Fiacre walked around the piece of land that he wanted, dragging his spade along. Wherever the spade touched the dirt, trees and bushes were uprooted and the dirt was plowed instantly. His association with making things grow made him a logical choice for the patron of infertility.

Generous Father, Lord of all things,
I implore you for the fertility of Fiacre.
Let this seed grow into a beautiful bloom.
Let children spring forth from this loving family.
Allow our harvests to be plentiful to share with others.
Pray with me, St. Fiacre, for the rich soil of life to nurture me.
Amen.

Isolation

St. Jane Frances de Chantal

Feast Day: December 12

J ane Frances Fremiot's mother died when Jane was a little over a year old, and she was then raised single-handedly by her father. At the age of twenty, she married the Baron de Chantal, and they had four children together. Her husband was killed while hunting and Jane was a widow at the age of twenty-eight. With nowhere else to go, the young mother was forced to live with her father-in-law, who was known to be a very unpleasant man. In 1610 she founded the *Congregation of the Visitation* for widows and women who did not want to take on the complete life of the orders. Her religious order grew, and eventually Jane Frances de Chantal went on to found sixty-nine convents.

Loving Jane Frances de Chantal, please ask our dearest Lord
To protect all of those who have been isolated.
I pray for those without family and friends to support them
And for those in my life that I have
Kept far away from my heart.
Pray to our loving Father that those who are standing alone outside
Will find a kind shelter under the grace of God.
Amen.

Knee Trouble

St. Roch

Feast Day: August 16

Also known as Rock or Rocco, this French noble had a deep sympathy for the ill and the poverty-stricken. During a pilgrimage, Roch came upon a man who had the plague. Roch cared for the man and others afflicted with the deadly disease and performed a number of miraculous cures while aiding the stricken community. However, Roch fell victim to the plague himself and went off to die alone in the middle of a forest. A small dog that brought him food saved him, and he returned to France. Charged later with being a spy, the devoted Christian died in prison. He is often represented with a plague sore upon his knee.

St. Roch, sympathetic healer,
I beseech your prayers for these troublesome knees.
Ask the Lord to make them strong and nimble
So that I may partake of all the gifts the Lord has provided.
Pray that I may walk painlessly and rest comfortably.
I ask this in the Lord's name.
Amen.

Large Families

St. Ferdinand III

Feast Day: May 30

Ferdinand was the son of a Spanish king and became king himself at the age of eighteen. He married Princess Beatrice, and the couple had ten children together. He ruled justly and with a great reverence for Our Lady. When Beatrice died in 1236, Ferdinand married Joan of Ponthiers, and they had three children. A devoted Christian king, Ferdinand founded hospitals and monasteries, churches and bishoprics. He worked to change Spanish law into a system that was fair. As the father of thirteen children, Ferdinand strove to be faithful, uncorrupt and devoted to his family, country and faith.

Faithful St. Ferdinand, father to many,
I implore your prayers for this large family.
Ask God to keep us together in good times and in bad.
Pray that our support for each other is strong and unshakable.
Pray to our Lord that he holds each member close,
Reminding them daily that they are special and loved.
Pray that our big family is blessed, happy, strong and safe.
Amen.

Learning

St. Thomas Aquinas

Feast Day: January 28

Thomas was a dedicated scholar who later became a gifted and brilliant teacher. He studied in Paris with Albert the Great and became a priest three years later, in 1250. He wrote many commentaries and Bible-related works and was named regent of studies in Naples while working on the *Summa Theologica*. The Church was made better for his work, which organized wisdom, thought and scholarship methods under the basis of Christianity. His impressive studies were savored after his death in 1274, and Pope Leo VIII made his teachings mandatory for all theology students.

St. Thomas Aquinas,
I ask for your intercession for a blessed learning experience.
Pray that I find ease in the text, wisdom in the teacher
And enlightenment in the process.
I ask the Lord to bless this experience for me
So that I may gather knowledge readily and
Use that knowledge for the glory of the Lord
In your example.
Amen.

Lightning

St. Barbara

Feast Day: Formerly December 4

Imprisoned in a tower by her tyrant father, Barbara was a stunning girl born in the early third century. She was educated in her tower by many creative and intelligent tutors. Her education brought her to the decision to convert to Christianity. Her father turned her in to the authorities for her faith; they ordered him to kill her, but she somehow escaped. Unfortunately for Barbara, her father found her and tortured and killed her. He was immediately struck by lightning and fell to the ground dead.

Lord God Almighty,
As the light flashes in the Heavens
I pray with St. Barbara to keep all around us safe.
Let the storm pass quickly and without destruction.
I pray that power is restored to all in need
And pray for those who were hit hardest by the downpour.
Amen.

Loneliness

St. Rita of Cascia

Feast Day: May 22

R ita was a very religious child and visited the Augustinian nuns in Cascia regularly. But her call to serve the Lord was abandoned when her parents arranged her marriage to an abusive and angry man who worked as the town watchman. She and her twin sons lived under her husband's abuse for eighteen years, until he was killed in an ambush. She taught her sons forgiveness, and when they died she was grief-stricken. She entered the convent and lived there for forty years. The patroness of loneliness was a sad wife, a grieving mother and, in the end, a bedridden nun. However, through it all she was devoted to the Lord.

Sweet and loving St. Rita of Cascia,
I entreat your prayers in battling this loneliness.
Ask the Lord to enable me
To seek out those who need me,
The many who love me.
Ask God to help me feel that love
And hold it close to my heart
So that I never feel alone in His grace.
Amen.

Long Life

St. Peter the Apostle

Feast Day: June 29

B orn as Simon, he was given the name Peter (which means "rock") by Jesus Christ. Peter was one of the Twelve Apostles. He made his living as a fisherman until his brother Andrew brought him to Christ. Jesus held Peter is such high regard that he desired the Church to be inspired by Peter's solid character. Peter worked miracles in his travels with Jesus and became the first pope. He was crucified about sixty-four years after Christ was born and chose to be martyred with his head facing the ground because he felt unworthy to die in the same manner as the Lord.

Solid St. Peter, friend and brother to Jesus Christ,
I ask for your prayers to God for the blessing of long life.
Please ask Him to let me see my great-grandchildren raised into adulthood
So they can hear the lessons and stories only elders can tell.
Ask Him to let my friends and family live long in health and happiness
So that we can all live to serve Him through our days.
Amen.

Lost Articles

St. Antony of Padua

Feast Day: June 13

Born in 1195 in Portugal, Antony of Padua entered monastic life at the age of fifteen and joined the Order of St. Augustine. Stirred to be like the Franciscan martyrs from Morocco, Antony decided to dedicate his life to spreading the Word of the Lord. Antony became the patron for recovering lost items because of the celebrated story of his lost prayer book. The beloved volume went missing, stolen by a young monk. Antony prayed to find the lost book and suddenly an apparition came to the thieving monk, ordering him to return the property to Antony. The book was rightfully restored to its owner. Since then, throughout the ages, Antony has been looked to for aid in finding lost articles.

Dear St. Antony,
You are the patron of the poor and the helper of all who seek lost articles.
Help me find the object I have lost so that I will be able to make better use
Of the time I will gain for God's greater honor and glory.
Grant your gracious prayerful aid to all people
Who seek what they have lost—especially those
Who seek to regain God's grace.
Amen.

Lost Causes

St. Jude Thaddeus

Feast Day: October 28

Jude's father was a martyr, and his mother kindly stood at the cross and anointed Christ's body after his death. He was actually the nephew of Mary and Joseph, and it is said that he looked very much like his cousin Jesus. His patronage of impossible causes stems from confusion between him and Judas. Since early Christians prayed for Judas' help and not to Jude Thaddeus, devotion to Jude was "a lost cause." Jude was killed with a club and beheaded after his death in Persia during the first century. His relics were distributed in Rome and France.

Dearest cousin of Christ, St. Jude Thaddeus,
In this desperate situation I ask for your prayers.
It seems all is lost but I remain faithful in the Lord.
Ask him to hear my solemn prayer and provide the best outcome.
Brave and honorable, St. Jude Thaddeus,
I beseech your help in praying for this hopeless cause
So that in the end, God's will is done.
Amen.

Lost Keys

St. Zita

Feast Day: April 27

Zita was an Italian girl who went into service in the house of a rich manufacturer. She never left her servant position and worked hard while also leading a devout life. The other servants made fun of her devotion to prayer until they realized the depth of Zita's holiness. She was eventually made the supervisor of the household staff and was known for giving the master's food and clothes to the needy. Miracles replenished these items before she could be found out. She is often depicted with sets of keys, undoubtedly due to her profession and responsibilities of the house.

St. Zita, holy house servant and prayerful soul,
I implore your dedicated prayers
In finding this set of lost keys.
Ask the Lord to save me time
And point me in the right direction.
Through His grace, may they be found quickly and easily.
In His holy name, I pray.
Amen.

Love

St. Valentine

Feast Day: February 14

Valentine was a Roman priest and doctor jailed for helping Christian prisoners. While he was incarcerated, Valentine converted the jailer by curing his daughter's blindness. There are various theories about how Valentine's Day began, one being that his feast day was a time when birds chose their mates. Another suggests that there was a mid-February pagan custom where boys wrote down girls' names to honor the fertility goddess. Saints like St. Valentine were called upon to Christianize the pagan custom, and zealots wrote the names of these saints instead. His feast day is connected to love, good marriages, affianced couples and young lovers.

St. Valentine of Rome,
Please pray for this love I have.
Let it saturate the earth with warmth and beauty,
Kindness and generosity, healing and safety.
Pray to the Lord that my love always remains true.
I ask for this romance to be kindled with God's love.
St. Valentine of Rome, in the Lord's name
Sing your loving prayers to Heaven and back.
Amen.

Marriage Problems

St. Helena

Feast Day: August 18

Born in the middle of the third century, her full known name was Flavia Julia Helena Augusta. Helena married the co-regent of the Western Roman Empire, and they had a son, Constantine the Great. Her marriage took a horrible turn when her husband left her to marry a woman who was more politically suitable. When he died, Constantine took the throne and treated his mother as royalty. When she was eighty years old, she went to the Holy Land to look for the True Cross and found it in 326. She built a church on the spot where it was located.

For the grace of a solid and loving marriage
I ask St. Helena to help.
Pray for us so that we make it through the rough times.
Ask God to bless our holy bond of matrimony.
St. Helena, I implore your prayers for the good of our marriage.
God, grant us the wisdom and the strength to make it work.
Amen.

Mental Illness

St. Eustochium of Padua

Feast Day: February 13

Born Lucrezia Bellini to a nun who had been tricked into ignoring her vow of celibacy, Eustochium of Padua was also known as the Cinderella of the Cloister. She spent her childhood in the convent and grew to find the calling to serve in a religious capacity. She entered the Benedictine order in 1461 and suffered for four years with outrageous and brutal hysterical attacks. She was thought to be possessed, and the other sisters took poor care of her during these times. When the abbess got sick, the townspeople thought it was Eustochium who'd poisoned her. The young nun died soon after taking her vows, and the name "Jesus" was found burned into her chest.

St. Eustochium of Padua,
Remind me when the mind is confused to look to the Lord.
When the brain is fevered, I must look to the Lord.
When madness creeps in, I offer my prayers to the Lord.
St. Eustochium, you felt the Lord's love through difficult moments.
I thank Him for continuing progress and the strength
needed to keep trying.
Amen.

Miscarriages

St. Eulalia

Feast Day: December 10

Born around 290 in Spain, Eulalia knew from an early age that she wanted to be a martyr for her faith. No one is sure if she was the Eulalia of Barcelona or of Merida, as both cities claim her as their own and their stories are quite similar. In Eulalia's early teenage years, Diocletian was persecuting Christians. Eulalia felt she needed to confess her true religion. Alone, she went to the tribunal and told the authorities there that she was a Christian. They tortured Eulalia in various ways before burning her alive at the stake. Dying so young has probably been a factor in her patronage against miscarriage.

St. Eulalia, who left this world as a peaceful child,
I implore your prayers for this unborn baby.
Ask our loving Lord to watch over this tiny soul
So that life continues and a beautiful future is certain.
We can pray together for a good beginning
To a long and healthy life.
Amen.

Misfortune

St. Agricola of Avignon

Feast Day: September 2

Raised in a religious family, Agricola's father was Magnus, a future saint. Agricola became a monk at the age of sixteen, was ordained and then became co-bishop with his father in 660. He built a church and a convent in Avignon, France, and employed his brother monks to run the two religious bodies. Ten years later he became bishop and was especially known for his charity and aid to the poor and disabled. It is believed his prayers prevented an invasion of birds in Avignon and also helped deliver rain, sunshine and bountiful harvests. Because his powerful prayers helped prevent disaster and brought good fortune for the farmers of Avignon, he has traditionally been called upon to intercede.

We pray to You, Lord God, for good things in our lives,
For health and success and for enduring love.
We look to You, Lord, to run our lives smoothly.
We ask St. Agricola to help us in our prayers to You
For continuing blessings on our family and friends.
We ask that You protect us from misfortune
And look upon us with compassion.
Amen.

Missionaries

St. Francis Xavier

Feast Day: December 3

Francis Xavier was a priest from Javier, Spanish Navarre, who became the first Jesuit missionary. While waiting in India for his ship to take him on his conversion missions, he preached along the streets in Goa and taught children their catechism and eventually converted the whole city. He baptized more than forty thousand people in India, the East Indies and Japan and endured horrific conditions on his journeys. He traveled barefoot and performed miracles as he healed and helped the sick and forgotten along the way. He died of a fever in China while on a mission journey.

Beloved St. Francis Xavier,
I ask for your prayers in defending the missionaries
Who are working so diligently in His service.
Ask God to inspire others to follow in their selfless footsteps,
Beseech the Lord to offer them assistance when they need help
And supply them with strength and insight at the necessary moments.
Pray they are kept safe so they may continue to spread His love.
Amen.

Money Managers

St. Matthew the Apostle

Feast Day: September 21

As a Roman tax collector, Matthew was considered to be a traitor by those he collected money from. For this reason, friends and followers of Jesus were shocked to see him associate with Jesus. According to legend, Jesus saw Matthew sitting at the tax office and asked him to follow. Matthew followed, not just in step but also in his way of life. He preached among the Jewish people for well over a decade, and he may have traveled to Ethiopia and farther east. His patronage is associated with accountants, bankers, bookkeepers, financial officers and stockbrokers.

St. Matthew, faithful servant to our Lord,
You toiled with coins and worked hard at your profession.
Ask the Lord our God to be at my side as I work in same regard.
I pray for good wisdom, good fortune, wise decisions and ethical practice.
May I see ways in my profession to make the world better.
I ask this through Christ our Lord.
Amen.

Motherhood

St. Mary, Blessed Virgin

Feast Day: January 1

M ary is the blessed and sacred mother of Jesus and the earthly wife of Joseph. It is thought that she was born around 20 B.C. She was a perfect mother to her holy Son and raised Him in sheer bliss. God chose her for her loving and tender nature, her patience, virtue and grace. She supported Jesus through persecution and stood by His side during His last days on earth. The Blessed Mother has many patronages but, of course, as the mother of Christ, she is most closely associated with motherhood. She is known to appear to people who are devoted and desire her prayers.

Dear Blessed Virgin Mary,
I humbly ask for your powerful prayers
For God's guidance in raising my children.
By your example, I strive to be a good mother
And teach my children right from wrong.
I ask your Son for patience, wisdom, strength and direction
In all the decisions I make for my children.
Sweet Mary, I need your prayers this day.
Amen.

Nervous Diseases

St. Bartholomew the Apostle

Feast Day: August 24

One of the Twelve Apostles, it is believed Bartholomew was introduced to Jesus by his very close friend Philip. He is mentioned along with Philip in the Gospels, and it is also thought that Bartholomew may have penned one of the Gospels that were ultimately lost. He became one of Jesus' disciples and traveled throughout Asia Minor, Ethiopia, Armenia and India spreading the Lord's Word. He endured a horrible death at Albanopolis in Armenia, where he was skinned alive. A patron saint of leather workers, tanners and cobblers, he is also considered the patron saint who is most helpful in praying for those with nervous disorders.

In His glorious and loving name,
I ask God for a healing, a blessing, and another day of strength.
St. Bartholomew, please pray for this poor soul who needs God's attention.
Ask that the suffering be lessened and the volatile situations be abolished.
Pray for the family and friends of the afflicted
That they may continue to help, love and survive this ordeal.
Amen.

Night Fears

St. Giles

Feast Day: September 1

Giles was born to wealthy parents in Greece, and when they passed away he used his money to aid the poor and destitute. He later moved to France, where he went into reclusion in a cave veiled by a thornbush. Giles prayed and meditated there for many years, giving his thoughts and heart to Christ. The darkness of his hidden retreat outside the city limits may be the basis of his patronage against the dread of night. He later left the cave and built the monastery of Saint Gilles du Gard and performed various miracles.

Dear St. Giles,
You embraced the darkness of night
And never let fear overtake you.
Pray for me so that I may find peace
As the light of day recedes.
Ask our merciful Lord to watch over me
So that I awake strengthened and inspired by the night.
Amen.

Oversleeping

St. Vitus

Feast Day: June 15

Of Sicilian heritage, Vitus was raised a pagan but was converted to Christianity by his tutor and his nurse when he was twelve years old. His father, a senator named Hylas, was so enraged at his son's shift in faith that he had all three arrested and scourged. It is believed they were freed from jail by angels only to be imprisoned again in Rome. Tortured and condemned to die, Vitus was thrown to the lions, but they did not attack. He was then thrown into a cauldron of boiling oil, along with a rooster, as part of a pagan ritual. The rooster's connection to rising early led to the young man's patronage and protection against oversleeping.

St. Vitus, I beseech your prayers.
Ask the Lord to help me rise on time each and every day.
With the Lord's blessing, please pray that I do not sleep too long
And can approach all of my mornings with time to spare.
St. Vitus, I ask for your help in this imperative request
So that I may not miss anything the Lord has in store for me.
Amen.

Pain

St. Madron

Feast Day: May 17

Madron was of Cornish descent and lived as a hermit in the sixth century. Not much is known about him; however, it is thought that he was either a local man who accompanied St. Tudwal to Brittany or a disciple of St. Kieran. Madron died in Land's End, Cornwall, around 545 and has since been the patron of many churches, including St. Madron's in Cornwall, where there is a well of healing water that springs from the marshy ground. It is believed that by leaving a piece of cloth or a garment on the trees surrounding the well, miraculous cures can be attained. As the cloth disintegrates, pain gradually vanishes.

St. Madron, I leave a piece of me
Behind with good intentions.
I leave my pain behind
And offer it up to the Lord.
I implore your prayers, St. Madron,
That I may be free from hurt.
Please ask our Father for relief
And comfort on my behalf.
Prayerful saint, I respectfully combine my prayers with yours.
Amen.

G. F. STAAL   Geoffroy sc.

Parenthood

St. Louis IX

Feast Day: August 25

Born in 1214 to Louis VIII and Blanche of Castile, Louis aspired to be a model Christian prince and succeeded. He ruled at a young age after his father died and married the daughter of the count of Provence. The devout Christian and his wife, Margaret, had eleven children. He was aggressive in bringing what he thought to be a strong moral order to his subjects, leading by example with acts such as wearing a hair shirt beneath his robes to curb his lustful nature. He died in 1270, and many miracles have occurred at his tomb.

St. Louis, parent and king,
I ask for your prayers as I raise this child.
Ask the Lord for courage, wisdom, strength and peace
As I make important decisions that affect this child's life.
Ask our gracious Lord to guide me so that I never act out of anger or spite
And that I guide my child with the loving hand of a wise
and caring parent.
Pray that all mothers and fathers parent in God's light.
Amen.

Peace

St. Barnabas

Feast Day: June 11

A bearded, middle-aged apostle, Barnabas was considered a good and faithful man, and was a friend to Paul. The two men went on numerous missions spreading the Word of the Lord. They came dangerously close to being killed for what they believed in, but Barnabas and Paul managed to escape with their lives. They had a substantial falling out at one point and went their separate ways. Paul took Silas as his traveling companion, and Barnabas turned to John Mark. It wasn't until much later that the two reconciled and made peace with each other. Barnabas is often portrayed in art with an olive branch, a symbol of peace.

Peace and love, St. Barnabas, is what I pray for.
May I offer the olive branch
At a crucial time as you did with Paul.
Pray that I do what is right, not only what is easy.
I look to you, St. Barnabas,
To pray with me for a peaceful reconciliation
As we bow our heads in thanks to the Lord for all that He provides.
In the name of God, I pray for the strong character
To be forgiving at all times.
Amen.

Rape Victims

St. Joan of Arc

Feast Day: May 30

Joan was a French shepherdess and mystic completely dedicated to her Christian beliefs. From the time she was thirteen she was blessed with visions from saints, including Margaret of Antioch, Catherine of Alexandria and Michael the Archangel. In the early fifteenth century, England overtook France. Inspired by a vision, Joan went into battle with a banner that read "Jesus, Mary" and led troops to fight for France's freedom. Ultimately, she was captured by the Burgundians and sold to the English. The English tried her in court and she was executed as a heretic. She was retried and acquitted, but she had been dead already for twenty-three years. Her patronage of rape victims can be attributed to the suffering she endured during her execution.

Maid of Orleans, St. Joan of Arc,
Your prayers are needed for this poor soul who has been accosted.
Pray that she finds peace and courage to get through this terrible ordeal.
Ask the Lord to give her the bravery that you found in battle.
May God provide her with support from family and friends
And instill upon her a warmth and gentleness that she may have lost.
In His powerful name we pray.
Amen.

Respiratory Problems

St. Bernadine of Siena

Feast Day: May 20

A friar and a priest, Bernadine was also considered a great theological writer in the first half of the twentieth century. He was a powerful preacher and converted countless people to the Christian faith with his speaking skills. Thousands of people congregated to hear him speak of the Lord, and the events usually led to mass reconciliations during the unstable political times. His strong and charismatic voice was a basis for his patronage of hoarseness and respiratory ailments. He died in 1944 in Italy, bound to his code of honor and remembered for his peacekeeping and preaching skills.

St. Bernadine of Siena, you spoke to the masses.
I beseech your prayers to our Father to heal my lungs.
Ask Him to make my breath come easy,
My voice stay strong and my chest remain clear and calm.
Through your powerful prayers, ask Him to place his hand upon my chest
And empty my lungs of everything impure.
May my lungs be filled with only the song of His praise.
Amen.

Seasickness

St. Erasmus

Feast Day: June 2

There are hardly any facts available regarding Erasmus's life, but there are varied legends surrounding him. Also known as Elmo and Ermus, among many other names, he became the patron saint of sailors and seasickness, usually depicted in art with a windlass wound with a coiled rope. Stories about him multiplied on ships having crews of many different nationalities. The blue electricity drawn to a ship's mast during thunderstorms, called "St. Elmo's fire," was thought to have been proof of his protection. The eerie atmospheric electricity comforted sailors during storms and, by any of his names, Erasmus is called on by those set upon the sea.

Saint of the sea, protector of sailors,
Ask our God to keep me steady on the waves, strong and quick on my feet.
May the weather be calm and the waves be kind
As we chart our course toward our destination.
Protect those who make a living on the water
And those who merely find peace far from shore.
Bless the vessel that it may guide us home safely.
Amen.

Sexual Temptation

St. Mary Magdalene

Feast Day: July 22

M ary Magdalene was one of Jesus' most faithful followers. According to the Bible, she had been a sinner and Christ drove the evil from her. Because of the Lord's kindness, she completely transformed her way of life. Her thanks to Him were shown by her love and complete devotion to God. She was present at our Lord's Passion and burial and was among the women who ministered to Christ during his suffering and actually washed his feet with her hair. She was also the messenger of the good news of Jesus' Resurrection. Mary Magdalene's example of penitence has inspired Christians for centuries.

O faithful Mary Magdalene,
You were so willing to atone for your sins,
Finding happiness and light through God.
I entreat you to pray for me so that I may rid myself of wrongdoing.
Pray that I remain true to God's desire and keep my own desires pure.
Ask our Father in Heaven to take away this temptation
So that I may remain on the path of righteousness.
Amen.

Sick Animals

St. Nicholas of Tolentino

Feast Day: September 10

Nicholas became an Augustine friar in 1263 when he turned eighteen years old. After becoming ordained at the age of twenty-five he had a vision that he was to move to Tolentino, Italy, and he remained there for the rest of his life. He had a strong devotion to the recently dead and prayed constantly for the souls in Purgatory. It is said he resurrected over one hundred children, including a number of children who had drowned together. He was once served a roasted fowl and the priest made the sign of the cross over it. It immediately came back to life and flew out the window. Nicholas was a vegetarian, and perhaps that, combined with the story of the fowl, is why he is the patron saint of sick animals. He died in 1305 after a lengthy illness.

St. Nicholas of Tolentino,
Lover of animals and healer of the sick,
I beseech your prayers for this poor suffering pet.
The Lord understands the role this animal plays in our family
And how our lives would be empty without our friend.
Ask the Lord to relieve its pain so it can enjoy life
with our family once again.
St. Nicholas, I ask for your help in the name of the Lord.
Amen.

Sick Children

St. Clement I

Feast Day: November 23

The fourth pope, Clement I was also referred to as Clement of Rome. He succeeded Cletus and may have personally known the apostles Peter and Paul. Highly regarded in the Church, Clement's authority restored order in the Church at that time. As a writer, Clement was the first Christian to associate the myth of the phoenix with the Resurrection. He was considered an extremely holy man who was dearly close to God. For this reason, a prayer offered by Clement can be considered especially strong. He died around the beginning of the second century as a martyr.

Pope and prayerful soul,
I call on you, St. Clement, for your help in this request.
Pray unto the Lord with me for the healing of this sick child.
Ask the Lord to take away the suffering and make this young soul healthy.
Ask Him to keep the family strong through this exhausting battle.
Clement, I call on you for your influential prayer
So that this child will be well again and may live a long and healthy life.
Amen.

Skin Disease

St. George

Feast Day: April 23

George is most well-known for the *Golden Legend*. According to the story, a dragon lived in a lake in Libya in the second or third century. Armies had tried to kill the beast, but they had been crushed in defeat. The dragon ate the village's only supply of food and when that was gone, the creature turned to devouring maidens in the town. George rode into the community and heard of the village's plight. He blessed himself with the sign of the cross and faced the dragon, killing it with one swift blow of his lance. He then converted everyone in the village into Christians and rode away. His story was quite popular in tenth-century Europe, and he is associated with knights, equestrians and skin diseases.

Known as the Bringer of Victory, you destroyed a hideous beast.
I beg of you, St. George, to pray for this irritation to be cured.
Ask God to take away the blemishes and the unsightly affliction
So that I may feel whole and healthy once again.
Give me the courage to enter the world
And ignore the eyes that fall upon me.
Give others compassion as I walk by.
In the Lord's name I pray.
Amen.

Stepparents

St. Leopold III

Feast Day: November 15

B orn into a noble royal family, Leopold succeeded his father at the age of twenty-three to become the military governor of Austria. He married a widowed single mother of two who was the daughter of Emperor Henry IV. Leopold was a gentle and loving stepfather, and he and Agnes proceeded to have eleven children of their own. His stepson Conrad III became king of Germany. Leopold was a devoted Christian and worked tirelessly for his faith, founding the Benedictine, Cistercian and Augustinian houses in 1106. Although religious, he reportedly refused the throne of the Holy Roman Emperor in 1125. Leopold was active in support of the First Crusade and died in 1136 in Austria.

St. Leopold, stepfather to a king, father to many,
Your prayers are desired to help this family.
Ask Jesus Christ, our Lord and Savior,
To bless all the people who love other children like their own.
Ask God to give them the support they need to be loving
and generous parents.
Let God guide children toward accepting their stepparents
And make them open to love and respect for all.
Amen.

Stomach Disorders

St. Bonaventure

Feast Day: July 15

Bonaventure was born in Tuscany, Italy, in 1221. As a child he was very ill and, through the prayers of Francis of Assisi, he was cured of his childhood affliction. At the age of twenty-two, Bonaventure became a member of the Franciscan Order of Friars Minor. He traveled to France and spent much of his time studying philosophy and theology in Paris. He became a trusted friend of Thomas Aquinas and King Louis, both future saints themselves. In 1256, Bonaventure was named general of the Franciscan order and that same year was a speaker at the Council of Lyons. Unfortunately, Bonaventure passed away before the close of the Council in 1274.

Blessed St. Bonaventure,
I ask for your sympathetic prayers
Because you know this kind of disorder well.
Pray with me for comfort and healing in the hands of the Lord.
Ask Him to make me well and able to wake up each day
With the strength and courage needed to continue with His plan.
Our prayers together can work a miracle with the Lord.
Amen.

Storms

St. Scholastica

Feast Day: February 10

Scholastica and her twin sister, Benedict, were born in 480, and their mother died while giving birth to the girls. She became a nun and completely devoted herself to the spiritual life. Scholastica had a brother who was also quite spiritual, and they would visit once a year. During his visit in 543, they spoke of God and other holy matters. They talked long into the night, and Scholastica asked him to stay until morning so they could continue their divine conversation. When her brother said he had to return home, the Heavens suddenly opened and a storm unleashed a horrible fury, preventing his departure. Scholastica told him that God also wanted him to stay with her that night, and so he did. Three days later, he saw Scholastica's soul leave her body in the night and turn into a dove as it entered the Heavens.

Devoted spiritual saint,
I pray with you for a calm in the air.
Let the damage be light and winds be tamed by the hand of the Lord.
Pray with me that all are safe during this powerful storm
And that our homes remain strong under its current.
St. Scholastica, I meekly ask for your prayerful help
In this dark and frightening hour.
Amen.

Students

St. Gregory the Great

Feast Day: September 3

Educated by the greatest and most knowledgeable teachers in Rome, Gregory was the son of a rich Roman senator and Silvia, who would later also become a saint. He grew up to be prefect of Rome and then, only a year later, sold all of his belongings and turned his house into a monastery. He built seven monasteries in Rome and Sicily and became a monk. When he witnessed children from England being sold in the Roman Forum, he became a missionary to England to put a stop to these horrific injustices. He was later elected pope and is also known as the initial collector of melodies and plainchant now known as Gregorian chants. The patron saint of students, Gregory's love for children and education was immeasurable.

St. Gregory the Great, father of the fathers,
I implore your prayers for all of the students who need guidance.
Pray they make their studies a top priority
And that their teachers are sound and committed.
Ask God to let the knowledge flow readily to their hearts and minds
And reward them for their sacrifice and dedication to their education.
Through the Lord, Jesus Christ, I pray this solemn prayer.
Amen.

Temptation

St. Catherine of Siena

Feast Day: April 29

Catherine was born on March 25, 1347, in Siena, Italy. She was the youngest child in a large Italian family and knew that she was devoted to God from an early age. When she was six years old, she had a fantastic vision of Jesus and the Lord blessed her. Catherine never forgot this image in her mind. Her parents wanted her to marry, but she refused on account of her desire for a religious life. Catherine became a Dominican tertiary, a mystic, and also manifested the stigmata on occasion. In a later vision she was married to Christ and the infant Jesus offered her a wedding ring as a symbol of this union. She died in 1380 of a mysterious illness.

St. Catherine of Siena, I call on you for help this day.
I pray to the Lord to keep me from going astray.
Pray with me to the Lord our God that I am responsible and true.
I ask His help, along with your prayers,
To remain steadfast, whatever the temptation may be.
St. Catherine of Siena, I ask you to give your glory
To the Father in Heaven and pray for me.
Amen.

Unborn Children

St. Gerard Majella

Feast Day: October 16

W hen Gerard was only twelve years old, the death of his father brought financial ruin to the family. The sickly young boy later tried to join the Capuchin order, but he was denied because of his health. He was, however, accepted into the Redemptorist order as a lay brother and served them in many ways as a gardener, tailor, porter and sacristan. His patronage of unborn children comes from a story about a woman who falsely accused Gerard of fathering her unborn baby. This lie upset Gerard greatly, but he retreated into silence about the subject. The woman later told the truth and cleared Gerard's name. Gerard was considered a wonder worker during his time with the Redemptorists. He died of tuberculosis in 1755 at the age of thirty.

St. Gerard Majella, your prayers for the unborn are so greatly needed.
I ask you to offer your prayers for the health and the future
Of such poor little souls who deserve every chance to survive.
Through God's will, pray for a safe pregnancy
And for the tiny being to grow and thrive in His love.
St. Gerard Majella, I humbly ask for your intercession
For all of the unborn in the world.
Amen.

Vanity

St. Rose of Lima

Feast Day: August 23

R ose was born as Isabel in Lima, Peru, in 1586. Her parents were Spanish immigrants, and they raised their daughter with love and devotion. She was a beautiful girl who offered herself to the Lord in a sincere vow of chastity. She was so committed to this vow that she used pepper and lye on her skin to make herself ugly and undesirable to men. She grew vegetables in her garden and did embroidery to sell to make money for her family and others who were less fortunate. She was a visionary and a mystic and was the founder of social work in Peru. She was also the first saint to be born in the Americas. Rose died in August 1617 in the town where she was born.

St. Rose of Lima,
Give me the vision to see beyond the mirror.
I ask for your prayers so that the Lord
Will see that I am kept grounded.
I pray with you that He will keep me humble
And remind me that I am merely His servant.
I ask that the vanity I am guilty of is dispersed with this prayer.
Amen.

War

St. Elizabeth of Portugal

Feast Day: July 4

The daughter of King Pedro III, Elizabeth was named after her great-aunt, St. Elizabeth of Hungary. She had a very devout upbringing in thirteenth-century Spain and devoted herself to constant prayer and religious education. She married King Diniz when she was twelve and became queen of Portugal. She had two children, and later there was a terrible conflict between her son and his father, the king. The two went into battle against each other and Elizabeth took it upon herself to ride a horse onto the battlefield, get between them and make them resolve their differences without going to war. This act became the basis on which Elizabeth was named the patroness of peacemaking and invoked during wartime.

As the conflict rages on, St. Elizabeth,
I call upon your holy prayers to bring peace to the people.
Ask of the Lord our God to put a stop to the killing.
Ask God to teach children to renounce the hate and violence
they see each day.
Through your prayers, ask God to give those who hate the most
The tools needed for a world of peace.
I beseech you, St. Elizabeth of Portugal, for your peaceful prayer.
Amen.

Widowers

St. Thomas More

Feast Day: June 22

Thomas More was born in London, England, in 1478. He was highly educated and worked as a page for the archbishop. Thomas became a lawyer and was able to use his intellect in various ways. He soon became lord chancellor of England, a position that made him second in power to the king. Extremely family oriented, he was married twice and was a loving father to his four children. Later in his career, his disagreed with the king on religious subjects, and it cost him his life. He was martyred in 1535 because he refused to give in to the king regarding his beliefs.

Offer a prayer, St. Thomas More,
For all the men who have lost their wives.
I ask you to pray for the souls left behind.
Ask our Heavenly Father to provide them with hope and courage
To continue living when the pain is more than they can bear.
Ask our God to offer them the chance
At new love and new life through God's will.
Amen.

Widows

St. Ludmila

Feast Day: September 16

Ludmila's father was a Slavic prince and grew up surrounded by political struggles. Born around 860, Ludmila married Borivoy, a Bohemian duke, when she was just a young teenager. She had six children with Borivoy, and the two built the first Christian church in Bohemia. Ludmila became a widow in 894 and gave up all of her material possessions after Borivoy's death, dedicating her life to serving God. She looked to her offspring and their children to save Christianity in Bohemia, and she went to great lengths to see this religious rescue through. Two men strangled her with her own veil on September 16, 921, for religious and political reasons. She was immediately called a martyr for her faith.

Widow and mother, St. Ludmila,
You did your best after losing your husband.
Your prayers are so important in helping other women find peace.
Through God's will, we pray for the ladies who find themselves alone.
We pray that they find the courage to see through the darkness
And to remember that the Lord is always by their side.
St. Ludmila, please pray they find strength and solace in God.
Amen.

Writers

St. Francis de Sales

Feast Day: January 24

Also called the Gentle Christ of Geneva, Francis de Sales was born in Savoy in 1567. His family was well-to-do and his parents wanted him to carry on the family's fine standing by becoming a lawyer and entering the political arena. He granted their wish, and after intense education he returned home a doctor of law and took a position in the Senate. However, Francis heard a voice one day that told him to leave everything he had worked for so he could follow the Lord. He joined the priesthood, and in time his family accepted his life change. Francis then became a writer and spiritual director in the district of Chablais, which is why he is considered the patron saint of writers.

May the Lord guide me and all those who write for a living.
Through your prayers, St. Francis de Sales, I ask for your intercession
As I attempt to bring the written word to the world.
Let us pray that God takes me in the palm of His hand
And inspires my creativity and supports my success.
St. Francis de Sales, you understand the dedication required in this profession.
Pray for God to inspire and allow ideas to flow.
In His name, let my words reflect my faith for others to read.
Amen.

26 St. Porphyry of Gaza
   St. Victor the Hermit
27 St. Baldomerus
   St. Anne Line
   St. Gabriel Possenti
28 St. Oswald of Worcester
   St. Romanus of Condat
   St. Hilarus

MARCH

1 St. David of Wales
  St. Felix III
  St. Swithbert
2 St. Chad
  St. Pontius of Carthage
3 St. Winwaloe
  St. Cunegund
  St. Gervinus
4 *St. Casimir of Poland*
  St. Peter of Cava
5 St. Mark the Hermit
  St. Ciaran of Saighir
  St. John Joseph of the Cross
6 St. Julian of Toledo
  St. Agnes of Bohemia
  St. Colette of Corbie
7 Ss. Perpetua, Felicity and
       Companions
  St. Teresa Margaret Redi
  St. John Baptist Nam Chong-Sam
8 *St. John of God*
  St. Felix of Dunwich
  St. Theophylact of Nicomedia
9 St. Frances of Rome
  St. Pacian of Barcelona
  St. Dominic Savio
10 St. John Ogilvie
   St. Simplicius
   St. Attalas
11 St. Sophronius
   St. Eulogius and the Martyrs of
       Córdoba
   St. Oengus

12 St. Pionius
   St. Innocent I
   St. Seraphina
13 St. Leander of Seville
   St. Heldrad
   St. Ansovinus
14 St. Matilda
15 St. Zachary
   St. Louise de Marillac
   St. Clement Mary Hofbauer
16 St. John de Brebeuf
17 St. Gertrude of Nivelles
   St. Gabriel Lalemant
18 St. Cyril of Jerusalem
   St. Edward
   St. Salvator of Orta
19 *St. Joseph*
20 St. Cuthbert
   St. Martin of Braga
21 St. Nicholas of Flüe
22 St. Nicholas Owen
   St. Paul of Narbonne
23 St. Turibius of Mogrovejo
   St. Joseph Oriol
24 St. Hildelith
   St. Catherine of Vadstena
25 St. Dismas, the Good Thief
   St. Margaret Clitherow
   St. Lucy Filippini
26 St. Peter of Sebaste
   St. Ludger of Münster
27 St. Rupert
28 St. Hesychius of Jerusalem
29 Ss. Gundleus and Gwladys
   St. Berthold
   St. Ludolph
30 St. John Climacus
   St. Osberg
   St. Peter Regalado
31 St. Stephen of Mar Saba
   St. Secundus
   St. Guy of Pomposa

APRIL

1 St. Agape
St. Chionia
St. Irene

2 St. Francis of Paola
St. Theodosia
St. John Payne

3 St. Richard of Chichester
St. Sixtus I
St. Mary of Egypt

4 *St. Isidore of Seville*
St. Plato
St. Peter of Poitiers

5 St. Vincent Ferrer
St. Gerald of Sauve-Majeure
St. Eva of Liège

6 St. Prudentius
St. William of Eskill
St. Peter of Verona

7 *St. John Baptist de La Salle*
St. Herman Joseph
St. Henry Walpole

8 St. Julie Billiart
St. Dionysius of Corinth
St. Walter of Pontoise

9 St. Waldetrude
St. Casilda
St. Gaucherius

10 St. Fulbert
St. Michael de Sanctis
St. Magdalene of Canossa

11 St. Stanislaus of Cracow
St. Barsanuphius
St. Gemma Galgani

12 St. Julius I
St. Zeno
St. Joseph Moscati

13 St. Martin I
St. Carpus
St. Papylus

14 St. Tiburtius
St. Valerius
St. Lydwina of Schiedam

15 St. Paternus of Wales
St. Paternus of Avranches
St. Ruadham

16 St. Drogo
St. Benedict Joseph Labre
St. Bernadette

17 St. Simeon Barsabae
St. Donnan and Companions
St. Robert of Chaise-Dieu

18 St. Alexander of Alexandria
St. Laserian
St. Ursmar

19 St. Leo IX
St. Geroldus
St. Alphege of Canterbury

20 St. Anicetus
St. Hildegund of Schönau
St. Agnes of Montepulciano

21 St. Anselm
St. Apollonius
St. Anastasius I of Antioch

22 St. Soter
St. Caius
St. Leonides

23 *St. George*
St. Gerard of Toul
St. Adalbert of Prague

24 St. Fidelis of Sigmaringen
St. Mellitus
St. Mary Euphrasia Pelletier

25 *St. Mark the Evangelist*
St. Franca of Piacenza

26 St. Richarius
St. Paschasius Radbert
St. Stephen of Perm

27 St. Maughold of Man
St. Tutilo
St. Zita

28 St. Peter Chanel
St. Cronan
St. Cyril of Turov

29 *St. Catherine of Siena*
   St. Wifrid the Younger
   St. Hugh of Cluny
30 St. Pius V
   St. Erkenwald
   St. Joseph Cottolengo

MAY

1 St. Mafalda of Portugal
   St. Peregrine Laziosi
   St. Richard Pampuri
2 St. Athanasius
   St. Waldebert
   St. Antoninus of Florence
3 Ss. Philip and James
   Ss. Timothy and Maura
   St. Catherine of Kildare
4 St. Florian
5 St. Maximus of Jerusalem
   St. Hilary of Arles
   St. Angelo
6 St. Evodius of Antioch
   Sts. Marian and James
   St. Edbert of Lindisfarne
7 St. John of Beverley
   St. Flavia Domitilla
   St. Domitian of Maastricht
8 St. Benedict II
   St. Indract of Glastonbury
   St. Wiro of Utrecht
9 St. Pachomius
   St. Gerontius
10 St. Catald
   St. Solangia
   St. John of Avila
11 St. Majolus of Cluny
   St. Walter of L'Esterp
   St. Ignatius of Laconi
12 *St. Pancras*
   St. Epiphanius of Salamis
   St. Dominic of the Causeway

13 *St. Servatius*
   Ss. Mel and Sulian
   Ss. Argentea and Wulfram of
      Córdoba
14 St. Matthias
   St. Michael Garicoïts
   St. Mary Mazzarello
15 St. Vitesindus of Córdoba
   St. Isaiah of Rostov
   St. Isidore the Farmer
   St. Dympna
16 *St. Brendan the Navigator*
   St. Simon Stock
   St. Andrew Bobola
17 St. Paschal Baylon
   St. Madron
18 Ss. Theodotus and Companions
   St. Eric of Sweden
   St. Felix of Cantalice
19 St. Peter Celestine
   St. Ivo of Brittany
   St. Crispin of Viterbo
20 *St. Bernadine of Siena*
   St. Thalalaeus
   St. Ethelbert of East Anglia
21 St. Godric of Finchale
   St. Paternus of Vannes
   St. Theobald of Vienne
22 St. Julia
   St. John of Parma
   St. Rita of Cascia
23 St. Desiderius of Vienne
   St. William of Rochester
   St. John Baptist Rossi
24 St. Vincent of Lérins
   St. Simeon Stylites the Younger
   St. David of Scotland
25 St. Bede the Venerable
   St. Denis of Milan
   St. Mary Magdalene de' Pazzi
26 St. Philip Neri
   St. Eleutherius
   St. Mary Ann of Quito

27 St. Augustine of Canterbury
   St. Julius the Veteran
   St. Melangell
28 St. Justus of Urgel
   St. Germanus of Paris
   St. William of Gellone
29 St. Maximinus of Trier
   St. Bona of Pisa
   St. Andrew of Constantinople
30 *St. Ferdinand III*
   St. Joan of Arc
31 St. Petronilla
   Ss. Cantius, Cantianus and
      Cantianella

JUNE

1 St. Justin Martyr
   Ss. Pamphilus and Companions
   St. Wite
2 *St. Erasmus*
   St. Eugenius I
   St. Stephen of Sweden
3 St. Cecilianus
   St. Kevin
   St. Isaac of Córdoba
4 St. Petroc
   St. Quirinus
   St. Metrophanes
5 St. Boniface
6 St. Norbert
   St. Philip the Deacon
   St. Ceratius
7 St. Willibald
   St. Paul I of Constantinople
   St. Meriadoc
8 St. Maximinus of Aix
   St. Médard
   St. William of York
9 St. Ephraem
   St. Columba of Iona
   St. Andrew of Spello

10 St. Ithamar of Rochester
   St. Landericus of Paris
   St. Bogumilus
11 *St. Barnabas*
   St. Mary Rose Molas y Vallvé
   St. Paula Frassinetti
12 St. Antonina
   St. Onuphrius
   St. Ternan
13 *St. Antony of Padua*
   St. Triphyllius
14 St. Dogmael
   St. Methodius of Constantinople
15 *St. Vitus*
   St. Edburga of Winchester
   St. Bardo
   St. Germaine of Pibrac
16 St. Aurelian
   St. Benno of Meissen
   St. Lutgardis
17 St. Bessarion
   St. Hypatius
   St. Nectan
18 St. Amandus of Bordeaux
   St. Gregory Barbarigo
19 St. Romuald
   Ss. Gervase and Protase
   St. Deodatus of Nevers
20 St. Alban
   St. Silverius
   St. Adalbert of Magdeburg
21 *St. Aloysius Gonzaga*
   St. Eusebius of Samosata
   St. Méen
22 St. John Fisher
   St. Thomas More
   St. Paulinus of Nola
23 *St. Etheldreda*
   St. Thomas Garnet
   St. Joseph Cafasso
24 St. Bartholomew of Farne

25 St. Prosper of Aquitaine
   St. Prosper of Reggio
   St. Maximus of Turin
26 Ss. John and Paul of Rome
   St. Vigilius
   St. Maxentius
27 St. Cyril of Alexandria
   St. Samson of Constantinople
   St. John of Chinon
28 St. Irenaeus of Lyons
   Ss. Plutarch, Potomiaena and
     Companions
   St. Paul I
29 *St. Peter the Apostle*
   St. Paul
   St. Judith
30 St. Martial of Limoges
   St. Bertrand of Le Mans
   St. Theobald of Provins

JULY

1 St. Oliver Plunkett
  Ss. Julius and Aaron
  St. Shenute
2 St. Monegundis
  St. Otto of Bamberg
  St. Bernardino Realino
3 *St. Thomas the Apostle*
  St. Leo II
  St. Raymund of Toulouse
4 *St. Elizabeth of Portugal*
  St. Bertha of Blangy
  St. Ulrich of Augsburg
5 St. Antony Zaccaria
  St. Athanasius of Jerusalem
  St. Athanasius the Athonite
6 St. Maria Goretti
  St. Sisoes
  St. Palladius
7 St. Pantaenus
  St. Felix of Nantes
  St. Hedda

8 Ss. Aquila and Prisca
  St. Procopius
  St. Adrian III
9 St. Agilolf
  St. Nicholas Pieck and
    Companions
  St. Veronica Giuliani
10 Ss. Victoria and Anatolia
   Ss. Rufina and Secunda
   St. Amalburga
11 *St. Benedict*
   St. Pius I
   St. Olga
12 St. John Jones
   St. Ignatius Delgado and
     Companions
13 St. Henry II
   St. Mildred
   St. Margaret of Antioch
14 *St. Camillus of Lellis*
   St. Vincent Madelgarius
   St. Francis Solano
15 *St. Bonaventure*
   St. Donald
   St. Edith of Polesworth
16 St. Reineldis
   St. Fulrad
   St. Mary-Magdalene Postel
17 St. Kenelm
   St. Leo IV
   St. Hedwig of Poland
18 St. Philastrius
   St. Pambo
   St. Arnulf of Metz
19 St. Macrina the Younger
   St. Arsenius
   St. Symmachus
20 St. Joseph Barsabbas
   St. Aurelius of Carthage
   Ss. Flavian II and Elias
21 St. Laurence of Brindisi
   St. Victor of Marseilles
   St. Arbogast

22 *St. Mary Magdalene*
  St. Wandregisilus
  Ss. Philip Evans and John Lloyd
23 St. Bridget of Sweden
  St. Apollinaris of Ravenna
  St. John Cassian
24 St. Declan
  Ss. Boris and Gleb
  St. John Boste
25 *St. James the Greater*
  St. Christopher
  St. Olympias
26 Ss. Joachim and *Anne*
  St. Bartolomea Capitanio
27 St. Pantaleon
  St. Celestine I
  Ss. Aurelius, Natalia and
    Companions
28 St. Victor I
  St. Samson of Dol
  St. Melchior García Sampedro
29 Ss. Martha, Mary and Lazarus
    of Bethany
  St. Olaf
  St. William of Saint-Brieuc
30 St. Peter Chrysologus
  Ss. Abdon and Sennen
  St. Julitta
31 St. Ignatius of Loyola
  St. Fabius
  St. Germanus of Auxerre

AUGUST

 1 St. Alphonsus de' Liguori
  St. Exsuperius
  St. Peter Julian Eymard
 2 St. Eusebius of Vercelli
  St. Stephen I
  St. Thomas of Dover
 3 St. Lydia
  St. Martin

 4 St. John Vianney
  St. Ia
  St. Molua
 5 St. Oswald
  Ss. Addai and Mari
  St. Emydigius
 6 Ss. Justus and Pastor
  St. Hormisdas
 7 St. Donatus
  St. Victricius
  St. Albert of Trapani
 8 *St. Dominic Guzman*
  St. Cyriacus, Largus, Smaragdus
    and Companions
  St. Altman
 9 St. Romanus
  Ss. Nathy and Felim
  St. Teresa Benedicta of the Cross
10 *St. Laurence*
  St. Blaan
11 *St. Clare of Assisi*
  St. Susanna
  St. Equitius
  St. Gaugericus
12 St. Euplus
  St. Lelia
  St. Porcarius and Companions
13 Ss. Pontian and Hippolytus
  St. Maximus the Confessor
  St. Wigbert
14 Ss. Felix and Fortunatus
  St. Arnulf
  St. Maximilian Kolbe
15 St. Simplician
  St. Alipius
  St. Stanislaus Kostka
16 St. Stephen of Hungary
  St. Armel
  St. Roch
17 St. Mamas
  St. Clare of Montefalco
  St. Joan of the Cross

18 St. Agapitus
St. Helena
19 St. Andrew the Tribune
St. Sixtus III
St. Louis of Anjou
20 St. Bernard
St. Oswin
St. Philibert
21 St. Pius X
St. Luxorius
St. Sidonius Apollinaris
22 St. Sigfrid
St. Philip Benizi
St. John Wall
23 *St. Rose of Lima*
Ss. Claudius, Asterius and Neon
St. Eugene
24 *St. Bartholomew the Apostle*
St. Joan Antide-Thouret
St. Emily de Vialar
25 *St. Louis IX*
St. Joseph Calasanz
St. Genesius of Arles
26 St. Tarsicius
St. Maximilian
St. Anastasius the Fuller
27 *St. Monica*
St. Marcellus of Tomi and
    Companions
St. David Lewis
28 St. Alexander of Constantinople
St. Moses the Black
29 *St. John the Baptist*
St. Sebbi
St. Medericus
30 Ss. Felix and Adauctus
St. Fiacre
St. Margaret Ward
31 Ss. Joseph of Arimathea and
    Nicodemus
St. Paulinus of Trier
St. Raymund Nonnatus

SEPTEMBER
 1 St. Verena
St. Simeon Stylites
St. Giles
 2 St. Antoninus
St. Nonnosus
St. Agricola of Avignon
 3 *St. Gregory the Great*
St. Phoebe
St. Macanisius
 4 St. Marcellus
St. Ida of Herzfeld
St. Rosalia
 5 St. Bertinus
 6 Ss. Donatian and Companions
St. Magnus of Füssen
St. Liberatus of Loro
 7 St. Regina
St. Sozon
St. Stephen of Châtillon
 8 St. Isaac I the Great
St. Kieran of Clonmacnois
St. Thomas of Villanova
 9 St. Peter Claver
St. Gorgonius
St. Audomarus
10 St. Aubert of Avranches
St. Nicholas of Tolentino
St. Ambrose Barlow
11 Ss. Protus and Hyacinth
St. Paphnutius
Ss. Felix and Regula
12 St. Auilbe
St. Guy of Anderlecht
13 *St. John Chrysostom*
St. Marcellinus of Carthage
St. Maurilius of Angers
14 St. Maternus
St. Albert of Jerusalem
St. Peter of Tarentaise
15 St. Nicomedes
St. Valerian
St. Nicetas the Goth

16 St. *Cornelius*
St. Ludmila
St. Edith of Wilton
17 St. Robert Bellarmine
St. Satyrus
St. Lambert of Maastricht
18 St. Ferreolus
St. Richardis
St. Joseph of Copertino
19 St. Januarius
St. Peleus and Companions
St. Sequanus
20 Ss. Andrew Kim, Paul Chong
and Companions
St. Methodius
St. John Charles Cornay
21 *St. Matthew the Apostle*
St. Cadoc
St. Maura of Troyes
22 St. Phocas of Sinope
St. Maurice and Companions
St. Felix IV
23 St. Linus
St. Adomnán of Iona
24 St. Geremarus
St. Gerard of Csanad
St. Pacifico of San Severino
25 St. Aunacharius
St. Finbar
St. Ceolfrith
26 *Ss. Cosmas and Damian*
St. Colmán Elo
St. Nilus of Rossano
27 *St. Vincent de Paul*
St. Sigebert
28 St. Wenceslas
St. Laurence Ruiz and Fifteen
Companions
St. Exsuperius of Toulouse
29 *St. Michael the Archangel*
30 St. Gregory the Enlightener
St. Honorius of Canterbury
St. Simon of Crépy

OCTOBER
1 St. Thérèse of Lisieux
St. Romanus the Melodist
St. Mylor
2 St. Eleutherius of Nicomedia
St. Leger
3 St. Thomas of Hereford
St. Hesychius
St. Gerard of Brogne
4 *St. Francis of Assisi*
St. Ammon
St. Petronius of Bologna
5 St. Apollinaris of Valence
St. Galla
St. Magenulf
6 St. Bruno
St. Faith
St. Mary Frances of Naples
7 St. Justina
St. Mark
St. Helan of Cornwall
8 St. Pelagia the Penitent
St. Demetrius
St. Keyne
9 St. John Leonardi
St. Dionysius the Areopagite
St. Denis and Companions
10 St. Francis Borgia
Ss. Gereon and Companions
St. Mihršabor
11 St. Nectarius of Constantinople
St. Loman of Trim
St. Kenneth
12 St. Wilfrid
St. Maximilian of Lorch
Ss. Felix and Cyprian
13 St. Edward the Confessor
St. Maurice of Carnoët
St. Daniel and Companions
14 St. Callistus I
St. Justus of Lyons
St. Angadrisma

15 *St. Teresa of Avila*
   St. Thecla of Kitzingen
   St. Richard Gwyn
16 *St. Hedwig*
   St. Margaret Mary Alacoque
   St. Gerard Majella
17 St. Ignatius of Antioch
   St. John Kolobos
   St. Nothelm of Canterbury
18 *St. Luke the Apostle*
   St. Justus of Beauvais
19 Ss. John de Brebeuf and
         Companions
   St. Paul of the Cross
   St. Philip Howard
20 St. Caprasius
   St. Artemius
   St. Andrew of Crete
21 St. Hilarion
   St. Fintan of Taghmon
   St. Condedus
22 St. Abercius of Hieropolis
   St. Philip of Heraclea and
         Companions
   Ss. Alodia and Nunilo
23 St. John of Capistrano
   St. Severinus Boethius
   St. Ignatius of Constantinople
24 St. Antony Mary Claret
   St. Proclus of Constantinople
   Ss. Aretas and Martyrs of
         Najran and St. Elsebaan
25 Ss. Crispin and Crispinian
   St. Gaudentius of Brescia
26 St. Rusticus of Narbonne
   St. Cedd
   St. Eata of Hexham
27 Ss. Frumentius and Aedesius
28 Ss. Simon and *Jude Thaddeus*
   St. Fidelis of Como
   St. Faro of Meaux

29 St. Evaristus
   St. Narcissus of Jerusalem
   St. Theuderius
30 St. Serapion of Antioch
   St. Germanus of Capua
   St. Ethelnoth of Canterbury
31 *St. Quentin*
   St. Foillan
   St. Wolfgang of Regensburg

NOVEMBER
 1 St. Benignus of Dijon
   St. Caesarius
   St. Austremonius
 2 St. Victorinus
   St. Marcian
   St. Winifred
 3 *St. Martin de Porres*
   St. Rumwold
   St. Hubert of Liège
 4 *St. Charles Borromeo*
   St. Pierius
   Ss. Vitalis and Agricola
 5 Ss. Zechariah and Elizabeth
   St. Bertilla
 6 St. Illtud
   St. Melaine
   St. Leonard of Noblac
 7 St. Willibrord
   St. Herculanus
   St. Engelbert
 8 St. Cybi
   St. Deusdedit
   St. Tysilio
 9 St. Benen
   St. Vitonus
10 St. Leo the Great
   St. Aedh
   St. Justus
11 *St. Martin of Tours*
   St. Mennas
   St. Theodore the Studite

188

12 St. Josaphat
St. Nilus the Elder
St. Emilian Cucullatus
13 St. Brice
St. Maxellendis
St. Homobonus
14 *St. John Licci*
St. Laurence O'Toole
St. Dyfrig
15 St. Albert the Great
St. Leopold III
St. Raphael Kalinowski
16 St. Margaret of Scotland
St. Afan
St. Agnes of Assisi
17 St. Elizabeth of Hungary
St. Hugh of Lincoln
St. Gregory the Wonderworker
18 St. Philippine Duchesne
St. Romanus of Antioch
St. Mawes
19 St. Barlaam
St. Nerses
St. Nerses I
20 St. Edmund
St. Dasius
St. Bernward
21 St. Gelasius I
22 *St. Cecilia*
Ss. Philemon and Apphia
23 *St. Clement I*
St. Columbanus
St. Amphilochius
24 St. Chrysogonus
St. Enfleda
St. Albert of Louvain
25 St. Moses of Rome
St. Mercurius
St. Peter of Alexandria
26 St. Siricius
St. Conrad of Constance
St. Nikon "Metanoiete"

27 St. James Intercisus
St. Maximus of Riez
St. Fergus
28 St. Stephen the Younger
St. James of the March
29 St. Saturninus of Toulouse
St. Radbod
St. Francis of Lucera
30 St. Andrew
St. Cuthbert Mayne

DECEMBER

1 St. Edmund Campion
St. Tudwal
St. Ralph Sherwin
St. Alexander Briant
2 St. Chromatius
3 *St. Francis Xavier*
St. Lucius
St. Cassian of Tangier
4 St. John Damascene
St. Fare
St. Barbara
5 St. Sabas
St. Crispina
St. Sola
6 Ss. Dionysia, Majoricus and
Companions
St. Abraham of Kratia
7 St. Ambrose
St. Sabinus and Companions
St. Josepha Rossello
8 St. Eutychian
St. Budoc
St. Romaric
9 St. Leocadia
St. Gorgonia
St. Peter Fourier
10 St. Gregory III
St. John Roberts
St. Eulalia

11 St. Damasus I
   Ss. Fuscian and Victoricus
   St. Daniel the Stylite
12 *St. Jane Frances de Chantal*
   St. Finnian of Clonard
   St. Simon Hoa
13 *St. Lucy*
   St. Judoc
   St. Odilia
14 St. John of the Cross
   St. Nicasius and Companions
   St. Venatius Fortunatus
15 St. Valerian and Other Martyrs
      of North Africa
   St. Paul of Latros
   St. Mary di Rosa
16 St. Adelaide of Burgundy
17 St. Sturmi
   St. Wivina
   St. John of Matha
18 St. Flannan of Killaloe
   Ss. Rufus and Zosimus
   St. Gatian
19 St. Nemesius and Other Martyrs
      of Alexandria
   St. Anastasius I
   Ss. Dominic Uy, Stephen Vinh
      and Companions
20 St. Ammon and Companions
   St. Philogonius of Antioch
   St. Dominic of Silos
21 St. Peter Canisius
   St. Peter Thi

22 St. Frances Xavier Cabrini
   Ss. Chaerymon, Ischyrion and
      Others
23 St. John of Kanti
   St. Servulus
   St. Frithebert
24 St. Delphinus
   St. Tharsilla
   St. Mochua
25 St. Anastasia
   St. Eugenia
   St. Peter Nolasco
26 *St. Stephen the Martyr*
   St. Dionysius
   St. Zosimus
27 *St. John the Apostle*
   St. Fabiola
   St. Nicarete
28 St. Theodore the Sanctified
   Sts. Rumilus and Conindrius
   St. Antony of Lérins
29 *St. Thomas Becket*
   St. Trophimus
   St. Marcellus Akimetes
30 St. Anysius
   St. Egwin
31 St. Silvester I
   St. Zoticus
   Ss. Melania the Younger and
      Pinian

INDEX OF SAINTS